Strategic Procurement

For Howard, with love

Strategic Procurement

Organizing suppliers and supply chains for competitive advantage

Caroline Booth

KoganPage

LONDON PHILADELPHIA NEW DELHI

First published in Great Britain and the United States in 2010 by Kogan Page Limited

120 Pentonville Road	525 South 4th Street, #241	4737/23 Ansari Road
London N1 9JN	Philadelphia PA 19147	Daryaganj
United Kingdom	USA	New Delhi 110002
www.koganpage.com		India

© Caroline Booth, 2010

The right of Caroline Booth to be identified as the author of this work has been asserted by her in accordance with the Copyright, Designs and Patents Act 1988.

ISBN   978 0 7494 6022 8
E-ISBN   978 0 7494 6023 5

British Library Cataloguing-in-Publication Data

A CIP record for this book is available from the British Library.

Library of Congress Cataloging-in-Publication Data

Booth, Caroline, 1958–
    Strategic procurement : organizing suppliers and supply chains for competitive advantage / Caroline Booth.
        p. cm.
    Includes bibliographical references and index.
    ISBN 978-0-7494-6022-8 – ISBN 978-0-7494-6023-5   1. Industrial procurement. 2. Business logistics.   I. Title.
    HD39.5.B66 2010
    658.7'2–dc22
                                          2010013870

Typeset by Saxon Graphics Ltd, Derby

Contents

List of figures and tables

Preface

When you ask successful companies what has made them successful, very few will include, even on their long list, two rather neglected factors: third-party expenditure and suppliers. Yet I challenge you to think of any organization (successful or not) that doesn't have oodles of both.

For the last 20 years, one of the most enduring mantras for modern business has been 'focus on the core'. As a result, most companies now concentrate only on those activities that they regard as 'core' and rely on their suppliers to deliver the rest. This has, almost inadvertently, created a complex web of inter-company relationships that most businesses struggle to manage or exploit to their full potential. Therefore, and this is the scary part, very few organizations can truly claim to be in control of all aspects of their customer value propositions unless they are also competent at procurement and managing their suppliers. Yet how many business leaders see procurement or supplier management as key disciplines? Unless you are a manufacturer, the answer is very few. While procurement is increasingly recognized as a business discipline for its practitioners (complete with degree courses, thousands of books and recognized institutes), there is little real understanding of the true business value of procurement in boardrooms.

Providing a broad sweep across procurement, this book aims to fill this gap by concentrating on the 'why' and the 'what' of good procurement, and less on the 'how'. It explores procurement's strategic value to a business rather than the nuts and bolts of its implementation. As such I hope this book will be useful to executives and senior managers in helping them to better understand the often untapped value that better management of third-party spend and key suppliers can deliver to their organizations. I also hope that this book is useful to procurement professionals who want to better articulate their role in the success of the companies they work in, as well as those executives who manage them.

To put this into perspective, most organizations, regardless of industry, now spend more with their suppliers than they do on employing their staff. This means that they are buying business-critical goods and services that are intrinsic to their customer propositions. Company leaders need to recognize supplier relationship management as a key business lever and to reskill and reshape their organizations to manage their third-party spend and sources of supply. Reading this book will help the leaders of any company to better tap these valuable assets.

The typical situation in most organizations is that the percentage of resources ministering to its employees significantly exceeds the percentage managing their external third-party spend and key suppliers. It is time for organizations to move away from their traditional internal emphasis and refocus on the extended enterprises they have created and now need to exploit.

This book provides the rationale for any organization to redirect its effort to this neglected area of business. It is an area of rich rewards, where P&L impact is relatively painless and immediate, where benefit to cost ratios of 10 to 1 are realistic ambitions, where in-year payback is commonplace, and where both top-line growth and cost reduction are mutually inclusive.

Acknowledgements

I feel as though I have been preparing all my working life to write this book. Therefore I would like to thank everyone I have worked with over many years and across many companies for helping me to learn my trade and providing the experiences that contributed to it. Particularly I would like to thank Chris Miller who first opened my eyes to the world of procurement as my boss at Shell, way back in the early days of the North Sea, and Neil Maclean who kindly read and commented on the manuscript.

Naturally I want to thank my family for their enduring love and support and particularly my husband, Howard, who kept my feet to the fire when I would have happily put them up!

1 No company is an island

'We spend how much?' is a cry I have often heard from a senior executive the first time he or she finds out the true extent of his or her company's third-party expenditure.

Years ago, I asked the group finance director of a leading UK financial services company how much his organization spent with suppliers. He said that he didn't know but that it wasn't much because, 'we don't actually make anything. Don't forget, Caroline, we are a bank, not a manufacturer'. His company actually spent over £2 billion, and that was in the late 1990s. What this very capable executive had forgotten was that the bank had adopted (as most companies have) the business mantra that it should focus on its core and get other companies to take care of the rest. The bank therefore didn't print its cheque books, fill or service its cash machines, clean or secure its offices, but paid other companies to do it. Nowadays I could add to this list; for example, very few banks clear and process their own cheques. Several others are not even licensed by their central banks to distribute cash (a pretty fundamental process for a bank) but rely on another company to have that licence and do it for them.

What is interesting is that the motivation for outsourcing some of these critical processes is the mitigation of reputational risk in the event that something goes wrong. The perception is that if a supplier is fined by the central bank for a breach in the licensing agreement, this is less damaging than if it were the bank directly. Similarly in the North Sea's oil and gas fields, contractors are now responsible for some of the most critical offshore operations, not only because they have the expertise but because of the rather misplaced notion that if it all goes wrong, the public and the authorities won't blame the oil company.

I say 'misplaced notion' because, if I turn up at my bank's cash machine on a wet Friday evening and it is not working, I don't think, 'Oh that must be the fault of Manufacturer A because it makes the machines or Supplier B because it fills them with money, or Vendor C because it maintains the software.' Instead I think, and rightly so, that my bank has let me down.

It is my bank's responsibility to provide me with a reliable way of getting my money out whenever I want it. I don't care how they do it but I do expect and need it to be done well. Furthermore, any company that still thinks that it can shield itself from bad publicity when something goes wrong is naïve. The supplier may be responsible for the service but the procuring organization is always going to be accountable. Just look at British Airways in August 2005 when its catering supplier, Gate Gourmet, in an effort to reduce UK running costs, triggered industrial action both within its own company and in British Airways. This led to 900 flights being grounded, 100,000 travellers delayed, estimated losses for British Airways of £45 million and weeks of disruption where even after flights resumed there was no in-flight catering available. Less than three years later this unlucky airline faced similar public relations and economic damage when in March 2008 its dedicated and flagship Terminal 5 at Heathrow opened and suffered catastrophic problems. While the most serious were caused by the failure of the bespoke baggage handling systems, very few people know the names of the baggage systems providers, the construction companies or the programme managers – everyone remembers the airline.

What is third-party spend?

Third-party spend or expenditure is money paid to other companies in return for goods and services. It comprises three elements:

1. *Direct expenditure* – this term covers all goods and services acquired to be part of the good or service being created for sale. Obviously this is particularly relevant to manufacturing industry where, for example, more than 80 per cent of the cost of making a car is direct expenditure. It would also include all the bits and pieces

that go into a bank's added-value accounts where services are bundled with the bank account (eg travel insurance, breakdown recovery service), or replacement household contents by an insurance company.

2. *Enabling expenditure* – covers all goods and services acquired to allow the organization to fulfil its customer propositions but that don't as such go into the goods or services being sold. This is often asset-related – the offshore platforms of an oil company, the lorries and trucks of a haulier, the voice and data network of a telecommunications company, and the branch network of a bank. It also covers the research and development of a drug company or the sales and marketing expenditure of most organizations.

3. *Indirect expenditure* – covers all goods and services acquired to support the business. This is predominantly staff-related expenditure – property, facilities management, travel and entertainment, temporary labour, recruitment and personnel-related IT.

Interestingly, while automotive companies are often seen as the genesis of good procurement practice, their focus has primarily been on direct and enabling expenditure. It is only in the last few years that these companies have realized that there is real value to be harvested by also managing their indirect expenditure.

Different industries have different spend profiles, but in the majority of them third-party expenditure will equate to at least half of their costs. At one extreme sit the manufacturing companies (many having outsourced most of the manufacturing process itself) at circa 80 per cent, and at the other the oil and gas companies. While the percentage in oil and gas companies might be relatively small, the actual expenditure is still significant enough that a reasonable procurement improvement programme can impact their return on average capital employed by several per cent.

Supply chains

Management

You are probably wondering by now, what my beef is. If most organizations across all industries are already spending heaps of money getting other companies to do stuff for them – then surely, as a procurement person, I should be rubbing my hands together and thinking 'Job done!' In fairness I probably could, but not if I am thinking, 'Job done well!' And I suppose that is the nub of this book. Look at your own organization and ask yourself:

1. Are you happy with the service you are getting from your suppliers?
2. Are your customers happy with the service you are providing to them through your suppliers?
3. Do you know how to evaluate the quality of either 1 or 2?
4. Do you know why you asked your supplier to do that for you in the first place? Was it what you needed and will it still be what you need in a year's time when the contract is still running?

The reason I am asking these questions is that in all likelihood few if any in your organization have ever tried to ask or answer them. We train our managers to manage employees, not suppliers, and yet very few managers can deliver their primary business objectives now without relying on other companies. These other companies don't share your culture or priorities; they are almost never focused exclusively on you (and if they are you should worry even more); they don't understand your customers or your value proposition – so you have to wonder how they can ever truly, even with the best will in the world, do right by you.

There was a piece of research carried out some years ago by Dr Robert Monckza, Professor of Supply Chain Management at Arizona State University, which indicated that the further a supplier was from the end customer in a supply chain then the less that supplier understood the volatility of that supply chain – particularly in respect of changing customer requirements. If you consider the complexity of modern supply chains and ever-more fickle customers, this is pretty scary.

Customer and colleague supply chains

A supply chain is a series of activities that deliver an outcome to a recipient. That recipient may be internal (a colleague) or external (a customer). The activities may be undertaken by a variety of entities, once again both internal (eg your marketing department) or external (eg an advertising agency). Your supplier is unlikely to be doing everything you need and therefore will have other suppliers helping it. These tiers of suppliers are also important to the supply chain's outcome.

The major activities in a simple customer-facing supply chain are shown in Figure 1.1. Looking at this supply chain, you can overlay the specific activities involved in supplying most customer-facing goods (eg a mobile phone, a new drug or a car). Each supply chain will obviously vary from this the simple one – for example if this were the supply of a new car, some luxury car makers such as BMW and Mercedes would continue the supply chain into resale (as they make as much money controlling resale as they do selling the car first time around). With some tweaking, this supply chain could also cover a customer-facing service (eg a new bank account, insurance cover or broadband service).

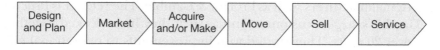

Figure 1.1   Example of a simple customer-facing supply chain

With a few more changes, a simple colleague-facing supply chain could be as shown in Figure 1.2. This would be a good starting point for most internally oriented goods and services such as a computer application, desktop services, office accommodation or security services. As we will see in a later chapter, one of the secrets of a good supply chain is determining the business need to be satisfied by it before specifying a solution. For example a business needs cold air, not necessarily an air conditioning unit – state the latter as your objective and you are already constrained (air conditioning is specifying how the need for cold air is satisfied) – but more of that later.

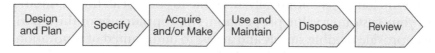

Figure 1.2   Example of a simple colleague-facing supply chain

Supply chain complexity

The supply chain, when it's laid out in this linear and rather graphic fashion, is obviously a gross over-simplification but it is a useful starting point for analysis. When you start to overlay business objectives, market conditions, customer demands, networks of suppliers and staff onto it, you can begin to understand why, unless you are very clear about what you are trying to achieve, it can all go horribly wrong. Also, hopefully, you should be able to see the opportunity: harness the power of your organization and its suppliers and deliver something amazing. Dell's just-in-time supply chain production line for its personal computers (PCs) is a great example. Dell is able to deliver PCs customized to each customer's requirements while keeping its inventories of finished products to near zero. Another is Wal-Mart's relationship with consumer goods manufacturers such as Proctor & Gamble. The retailer is Proctor & Gamble's largest customer, and as such they have worked together for over 20 years. They started with improvements to operational efficiency such as bringing together their point of sales and inventory replenishment systems and have since collaborated on product refinement and development initiatives to improve customer satisfaction and sales. All of these have improved the business performance of both organizations.

But even this isn't the true extent of the complexity of your business. Not only do you have to consider third parties that are suppliers to you but also suppliers that are your customers. Look at your list of creditors and debtors in your accounts payable and receivable – you could be surprised to see how many organizations are going to appear on both lists.

John Donne wrote that 'no man is an island'. In the 21st century to say that 'no company is an island' is equally appropriate and no less profound. To succeed in business is more complex than it used to be – it is no longer economically desirable to control all the components of your customer value proposition. Appropriate use of third parties can provide flexible supply and access to undreamed of innovation or new markets and scalability: all things that can make your business greater than the sum of its parts. However, it also requires additional and different management skills, and many organizations haven't really grasped this yet.

After spending half my life working with organizations helping them to improve, I am increasingly frustrated with my inability to get key messages across. For every CEO who gets it, another doesn't. For everyone who realizes supplier management is now a core skill, another will ask me how much we spend on pencils (the answer by the way is always 'not much'). For everyone who realizes how important it is to articulate his or her strategic intent another will say that he or she doesn't have time for strategy. And for any of you who are wondering why I am banging on about strategy in a book about procurement, I say read on: all will be revealed.

2 Know what your customers value

Years ago, a blacksmith smithed. The blacksmith would buy in the raw materials and was then responsible for everything to do with hewn metal – whether it was to make nails or a wheel rim. By the 19th century this situation was changing – machines were making nails more cheaply than the blacksmith could. So the blacksmith bought in the nails (and if he didn't, the owner of the hardware store did) and continued to make the wheel rims – for a while at least.

This simple tale is a good analogy for business generally. I can't think of any business that does everything for its customers any more – some hardly do anything at all. This raises lots of interesting questions such as, 'What is a company?' or if you want to personalize it, 'Why does my company exist?'

What I want to do in this chapter is stress the importance of understanding what your customers value about the products or services you provide, and will start looking at how best to satisfy their needs in the next chapter. Understanding your customer value is fundamental to answering that knotty philosophical question about your company's continuing existence. We are going to look at customer value because if you don't know why you are successful you are unlikely to marshal the right resources for the right outcome and therefore you are not going to be successful for very long.

Blindingly obvious you might say, yet a popular conceit in some companies is that customers value the things that their companies are good at doing. In reality this couldn't be further from the truth. Customers value what the product or service you offer enables them to do. Your company has a great value proposition if it allows your customers to do this thing that they value faster, better or cheaper than your rivals. Whether you do this yourself or get your suppliers to do it doesn't matter to your customers. However, you will come unstuck if you try to be faster, better or cheaper at something that does not and never will impact the things that your customers value.

You may think that I am straying from procurement here. But understanding and satisfying your customers is fundamental to good procurement. After all, I could save you a fortune and destroy what your customers most value.

Remember the iceman

One of my favourite business stories illustrates the importance of understanding what your customers value. It is about a company in the 19th century called the Tudor Ice Company. It was established in 1826 by Frederic Tudor, a wealthy Bostonian, and by the1860s was an international company exporting ice from the lakes in the north of the United States across the world to the Caribbean and even India. The industry was by then big business, with two in every three homes in Boston with ice boxes served by daily deliveries of ice. By the early 1900s the ice industry was in decline, challenged by source waters that were polluted by industrialization and urban sprawl. The final nail in the coffin was the introduction of domestic mechanical refrigerators around 1910 in the United States.

Commercial refrigeration had been available for several decades, and my question is, why didn't the company migrate into chemical and mechanical refrigeration at some point in the late 1800s when the writing for the ice industry was on the wall? The future of the Tudor Ice Company was undermined by its focus on what it was good at rather than concentrating upon what its customers valued about its product (Zasky, 2003).

As the company was really skilled at cutting and moving ice around the world – indeed it had several patents for just that – in the eyes of its owners its future looked rosy. While the Tudor Ice Company's core skills were in cutting and transporting ice without it melting away, its customer value proposition was extending the life of perishable goods and providing the opportunity to have the occasional ice cream. If the company had realized the latter was more important than the former it might have embraced refrigeration as the new and best way of satisfying its customers' needs.

This is illustrated by another anecdote about the Tudor Ice Company. When asked whether refrigeration was a threat to the company and particularly to its method of taking blocks of ice by horse and cart around major cities and delivering it to the housewives to put in their ice boxes, the owner said, 'No. Because what the housewives really value is the banter with the iceman as he delivers the ice to them.' This is a great example that once again illustrates the folly of failing to understand what customers truly value about your products or services.

For a very current example of this confusion we need to look no further than the internet. Since its earliest days one of the greatest challenges the users of the world wide web have faced has been their ability to retrieve pertinent information. In the early/mid-1990s many companies were created that focused on solving this problem. Companies like Webcrawler, Magellan, Excite, Lycos and AltaVista created catalogues of the web by using computer programs called 'spiders', which crawled from website to website indexing the pages. Other companies such as Yahoo looked to solve the same problem by employing a team of editors who reviewed websites and selected those suitable for inclusion in an A–Z directory.

Initially they were all successful because, despite the variable quality of their retrieval capabilities, they were the best in the market and there was a huge and growing demand. Backed by venture capitalists, one of the first challenges many of these companies faced was to find a way to make money, and ultimately most settled on internet-based advertising revenue. As a result a key objective of these sites was to keep users' eyeballs focused on the flashy adverts on their busy-looking web pages.

In the meantime, Sergey Brin and Larry Page, two students from Stanford University, identified a way to improve the retrieval quality of searches and created Google. Theirs was an ingenious and simple solution whereby the search engine ranked the number of times a site had been referenced (on the basis that good sites were accessed more often than poor quality or niche sites). They considered this as similar to the way in which the number of citations an academic paper receives indicates its importance (Nobel Prize winners typically are cited by tens of thousands of different papers).

Before Google formed as a company its founders met first with AltaVista, then Excite and finally Yahoo to figure out whether any of them had an appetite to buy Brin and Page's search technology for US$1 million. While these companies recognized that the technology was superior to their own, they rejected the offer because at that time no one thought that there was any way to make money from a search engine. The received wisdom was that advertising was the only way to make money, and these companies were focused on building websites that would keep users looking at their own pages where they could present adverts.

Conversely, Brin and Page believed their technology would fulfil a social need in making the information readily accessible to web users and they decided to make this their mission. So, having failed to sell their technology they established Google Inc with private investment and venture capital. To survive they still needed to make money and, ironically, advertising proved the best way to do it. They devised a way of delivering focused advertising that was driven by the customer's search keywords. When the customer typed in a search request not only did he or she get a ranked list of web pages, he or she also received a discrete list of adverts that might help satisfy his or her need. Indeed the adverts themselves were ranked by how frequently users clicked on them, and the less popular ones dropped down the ranking. In this way Google remained true to its mission of meeting its customers' desire for information relevant to their search request and yet still made money.

One could argue that Altavista, Excite and Yahoo had lost sight of what their customers valued (high quality information retrieval) and even who their customers were (the end users or the advertisers), whereas Google was intent on satisfying its end users' needs and found ways of making money while doing it. As Brin asked rhetorically, 'When somebody searches for "cancer", should you put up the site that paid you, or the site that has better information?' (Vise, 2005).

In 2004, six years after the company was incorporated, Google went public with an US$85 per share offer, raising US$2 billion in capital. In less than a year the price rose above US$300 per share. The rest, as they say, is history.

These examples show how important it is for a company to really understand its customer value proposition. The Tudor Ice Company thought its value proposition was the provision of ice (and perhaps even banter!) when its real value proposition was extending the life expectancy of perishable goods. Google on the other hand clearly understood that its customers wanted help to quickly find information pertinent to their searches. Furthermore, while it makes money from advertising, Google remains true to its customer value proposition by making sure that the advertising it provides is pertinent to the search itself.

Therefore your company's value proposition and the way you articulate it should have a huge influence on how you structure your company and will help to determine what you provide and what you source from others. I don't want to overcomplicate this, but I must mention that if you have more than one product or service offering in your organization you are very likely to have more than one customer value proposition.

Your customer value proposition

Einstein said that things should be as simple as possible but no simpler. This is the perfect mantra to keep in mind when figuring out your customer value proposition. I would like to add my own mantra to that of Einstein: keep it as vague as possible, but no vaguer. What I mean is that if you make your customer value proposition too specific you risk boxing yourself into a corner and in the process you could make yourself obsolete or redundant. However, if you make it too vague it could mean anything and everything and therefore will not provide the direction or focus that is so important. An illustration will help get my point across.

A mobile phone company shouldn't really see itself as a mobile phone developer and provider because what happens when mobile phones becomes obsolete – does the company? For example, its customer value proposition could be universal person-to-person connectivity. In this way the company will be interested in all aspects of interpersonal communication – regardless of the means of communication. Of course the challenge then is to determine where the boundaries are going to be for the company. Are the major competitors of the mobile communications industry going to be the fixed-line telecommunications providers or the computer manufacturers?

A well-articulated customer value proposition is therefore important for several reasons: it helps to future-proof your organization from both competition and substitution; it is a rallying cry for your own employees; it serves as a valuable litmus test when you are evaluating new ways of satisfying your customers needs; and it is a navigation aid to your suppliers, helping them to understand what 'good' looks like.

In summary

Figuring out what your customers' value now and in the future will help you to assess and select the best ways in which to satisfy them. This is fundamental to the success and longevity of your company. The good news is that you are not alone: when you are absolutely sure about what you need to deliver, there are lots of companies out there who can and will help you – these are your suppliers. In the next chapter we will explore this in more detail.

3 Right first time

In a perfect world you would be reading this book on the day you are starting a brand new venture. You have an absolutely killer value proposition, no existing infrastructure and a few key personnel: in essence a great idea and a blank sheet of paper. What a great opportunity to get it right first time! Right first time has a wealth of meaning and opportunity. Right first time means that you don't need to compromise because of things you are stuck with. Right first time means that you can implement the best possible supply chain and optimize costs from day one. In the real world things tend to work out slightly differently. This is probably because no matter where you are starting from, it is very difficult to start with a truly blank sheet of paper. There will be stuff on the page – even if it is written in invisible ink.

So what does this have to do with your supply chain and third-party expenditure? The glib answer of course is, 'everything'. When you have identified a new customer value proposition and are mobilizing to fulfil it there are lots of things that you need to make decisions on. Some of the most important of these will be what you are going to buy and from whom. Getting decisions right on what, if any, assets you are going to build and own and what components you will make or buy to deliver your new proposition are all key to how successful and how profitable the venture will become in both the short and longer term.

Don't forget that while value propositions can be huge (a new car, a new oil field or a new passenger aeroplane) they can also be something much simpler and smaller (a new savings product from a bank, a new style of mobile phone or new packaging for an existing product). So let's look at this in more detail and break down the opportunity in line with the types of goods and services we defined in the first chapter (direct, enabling and indirect). We will start with the most straightforward first – and the one that deserves least but often gets more time: the emotional spend – the 'indirects'.

Indirect or back office expenditure

This should get the least attention from the CEO and the management team and yet for some reason all too often it consumes vast amounts of time. Indirects are all the things that enable the organization to function – back office systems, accommodation, the dreaded stationery, etc. The solution should always be to get such things as cost-effectively as possible and ideally from the parent organization to ensure that you take advantage of economies of scale. If you must acquire these for yourself, seek providers that will deliver solutions – serviced accommodation, payroll services, etc. Your objective should be flexibility, speed and lowest cost.

There are lots of reasons why indirects become a millstone around the neck of a new venture. Let's take the case of a large company that decides to branch out into something new. It picks one of its best employees to lead the new venture and expects great things. The challenge is that the person chosen is best because he or she is talented and can make things happen in the current organization – which can be both a blessing and a curse. Where the new venture is still part of the company this might work out pretty well, but where the venture is a new company in new territory it is just as likely to end in tears. The reason is that the new company will take on some of the best and some of the worst of the old company. A 'large company mentality' can be a weakness if the new organization needs to be agile, nimble and lean, and especially if the new CEO expects segmentation of duties, with HR people doing HR and Finance doing finance: suddenly there is a millstone of lots of people in supporting functions that need to be paid for by an embryonic cash flow.

Worse still is the bear trap of 'entrepreneurialism' where the new CEO decides that after years of being forced to do things the company way he or she is going to break the mould and do things differently. No more shared services from the parent company; instead, if he or she needs some office accommodation – buy a building; back office systems – let's create some; stationery – no problem, get down to the shops; consultancy – just write the cheque. This is a CEO destined to be distracted by the back office.

This takes me back to the dot com days where some of the excesses of start-up companies were quite staggering. None characterized that era more than boo.com, a British fashion e-tailer started by two 29-year-old Swedish entrepreneurs. Before going bust, they reportedly spent US$188 million in six months building a brand name before selling a single item of clothing, with a large amount of that money spent on luxury offices, first-class plane travel and five-star hotels (Sorkin, 2000).

When I was being interviewed by Ernst & Young to join their management consultancy practice, I made the mistake of saying that I was keen to join them because I thought they were fleet of foot and entrepreneurial. The very seasoned partner looked at me over his glasses and said that he wasn't sure that 'entrepreneurial' was the right term. After some consideration he said that he thought that his firm was more 'entrepreneurialism with lead strings'. Lead strings are those harnesses that toddlers are put in by their parents so that they can charge off at their own pace – but remain about two feet ahead of the adult who is looking after them; or the harnesses that you might put on a team of horses to make sure they pull in the same direction. I think this is a great analogy for new ventures.

A new venture should draw succour from its parent organization where possible or a fit-for-purpose service provider if not, in all the areas that are not core to its new value proposition. Back office services, whether they are related to personnel, finance, property, procurement or admin should be a given. Sometimes the parent company makes this very difficult because of cost-recovery mechanisms like transfer charging, which can add a huge burden to start-ups. The parent should take into account that arbitrary recharging mechanisms can result in the wrong decisions being made, especially when some of these recharge costs are fixed and therefore are effectively sunk costs and with other ways to recover them. The CEO should focus on the company's value proposition and leave the rest to experts (whether that means the parent company or a supplier).

I remember talking to the country MD of a global IT company who said that when he joined as MD he was told that he had a choice. He could take the services from the group's shared services function (IT, finance, HR, procurement) and these would be 'free' to his balance sheet, or he could elect to buy these services from elsewhere, in which case he would have to fund them from revenues. Either way he was going to be judged on his P&L. He said it took him a nanosecond to sign up to the shared service model.

My advice on indirect expenditure is to take as much as you can from your parent company and if you do need to acquire other stuff directly, then buy services not goods and keep them vanilla – don't bespoke them. Indirects are the hygiene factor: you need them, but the success of your venture won't be because of them – but if you get too involved with them then your failure might be.

Direct expenditure

So now we have got rid of the distraction that is indirects, let's look at the heartland of what this venture is all about – the customer value proposition and how to satisfy it. This is your direct expenditure and covers everything that will be going into your product or service offer. Chapter 12 is going to go into this in a lot more detail, as picking the right goods and services from the right suppliers with appropriate contracts is worthy of some deeper study. However, there are some fundamental dos and don'ts in respect of direct expenditure that I want to touch on here.

The first is to ensure you consider very carefully what you make and what you buy. Once again there is a whole chapter on this later in the book. But it is also true to say that the decisions you make when addressing this question right at the start of your venture will have a more significant impact than any you make later in its life.

Tata Motors recently launched the Nano in its target Indian market. The project was dreamed up by Ratan Tata when, in 2003, he watched a young family – father, mother and two young children – balanced on a motor cycle. As Mr Tata observed, 'it led me to wonder whether one could conceive of a safe, affordable all weather form of transport for such a family' (Ray, 2008). What I think is interesting in this statement is that Mr Tata didn't once mention the word 'car'. This resonated with me because I have a friend in London who has invested £3,000 in a small electric car – to him he hasn't bought a car but instead has bought a replacement for his bicycle which, unlike his bike, will keep him dry on a rainy day. Any automobile manufacturer who thought my friend needed a car would not necessarily have developed anything that really suited him (such as the avoidance of the congestion charges in central London, free parking even at a meter and weaving in and out of traffic – although the last point might be just him!) because they would have been hidebound by everything they know about what a car should be (luxurious, capable of high speed, envy-generating).

Tata, despite owning Jaguar and Land Rover, didn't fall into this trap: it didn't price the Nano by adding up all the likely production costs and adding a margin. Instead it spotted a price point – just above that of the motorcycle it was planning to displace – and then worked with its suppliers to come up with a design that would enable it to hit the target price and still make a profit. After a few false starts it decided to ship the Nano as kit cars that could be assembled locally and in this way avoided all the capital needed for large final assembly plants as well as the associated follow-on costs such as assembly labour and transport for final products (Ferrari, 2009).

The suppliers it selected to work with were a mixture of traditional automotive suppliers (eg Delphi, a spin-off from General Motors that it has recently reacquired) and others (eg Bosch, which is best known for manufacturing appliances and motors). It kept revisiting its target customer needs while looking for cost-reduction opportunities (eg the engine is small because the traffic jams that are typical in Indian cities mean that transport mostly moves at average of 10 to 20 miles an hour) (Scanlon, 2009).

To achieve the target cost, Tata talked to potential customers to understand what they wanted and what they were willing to pay for it. This seems a great way of distinguishing between functions and features. A function is a must have, something that is intrinsic to the article (eg propulsion and something to sit on). A feature is something that might help the customer select between two competing products (eg metallic paint or a sun roof). The basic Tata Nano has functions; features cost extra. With a target market in India alone of between 50 and 100 million people, the Nano might be small but it has strong ambitions.

What this example demonstrates is that direct expenditure should be optimized to meet the needs of your target market and customer value proposition. Indeed I might go so far as to say that direct expenditure that doesn't meet the needs of its market and value proposition is wasted, and as such will at best reduce your profit margin and at worst might compromise the positioning of your product or service in the eyes of your customer. In this context 'function' needs to be the focus of your efforts and 'features' need to be tightly managed. Over time, features might become functions in a highly competitive market when evolution of your product is required to keep it fresh and attractive to its customers. However, features in a start-up can be as dramatic a distraction as indirect spend and can actually compromise the longevity of your product's attractiveness if you introduce them from day one. You only need to look at the products that have great longevity, such as PG Tips and various washing powder brands, to recognize the truth of this. Their manufacturers have lots of features (pyramid-shaped tea bags, soap capsules, balls and bubbles) up their sleeves, and deciding when to introduce them is as critical to their product freshness and market share as their development in the first place.

Enabling expenditure

One area where 'right first time' pays incredible dividends is when the new venture needs assets. One of the first decisions you need to make regarding any enabling expenditure is whether to lease or buy something. What in essence you are doing when you make such decisions is determining whether something is going to be a fixed or variable cost for your business. This is pretty fundamental and can impact your balance sheet for years – it is therefore worthy of considerable thought and should be scrutinized at the highest levels of your company.

Hopefully, having read the earlier sections of this chapter, you will realize that it is usually a very bad idea to buy an office to house your back office staff. If you need the accommodation at all then the best thing you can do is to lease or rent. This lesson applies equally to retail space, manufacturing plants, etc.

Assuming that this thought has resulted in a decision to own the assets, let's now look at the implications for that. I can best provide an illustration of this concept with examples of 'how not to' manage enabling expenditure.

If I had a dollar for every time someone has said to me, 'Don't worry about it, it's only capital expenditure', I would now be sitting on a beach in the Caribbean drinking cocktails. If these companies had even half-listened to my reply they would be even richer. And I say this for lots of reasons. For one, capital is still cash, and spending cash wisely is surely important to everyone. Second, capital expenditure (capex) gets ignored because its impact in-year on a company's profit and loss statement is limited to depreciation, but don't forget depreciation goes on for all the years of an asset's useful life. Finally, but most important, capital is creating a stream of operating expenditure every year the asset remains in use. A typical rule of thumb is that whatever you spend on an asset (whether it is software, equipment or physical infrastructure), you are likely to spend at least five times that amount on operating expenditure (opex) during its life – installing, financing, using, maintaining and ultimately scrapping it. This is known as 'the total cost of ownership', and I explain it in detail a little later in this chapter. So in my book: if you can choke capex, you starve opex. Alternatively, ignore capex and be prepared to pay the price year after year after year.

Just look at the North Sea. Oil exploitation in the North Sea started in earnest in the early 1970s just before the 1973 oil crisis, and by the middle of the following decade some important mistakes had already been made. Mistakes that mean that for much of the last decade the North Sea has been only marginally attractive and in decline. Indeed only the oil price and technical innovation are staving off the inevitable. In the late 1990s, when oil was languishing at US$11 a barrel I was involved in a pan-industry, government-backed task force that had the lofty remit of figuring out what better supply chain management could do to help prolong the life expectancy of the North Sea oil and gas industry. We came up with some great ideas, many of which are now standard practice in the region – but some of the core underlying problems remained because it was both too late and too expensive to tackle them. So what had happened?

I was lucky enough to be involved in the early 1980s in the construction of one of the North Sea's oil and gas platforms. The UK oil industry at the time was how I would imagine the Wild West in the United States was a century earlier – all about unfamiliar territory: exploring it, securing it, building on it and producing from it. The oil price was good, the UK government had awarded licences for blocks of the North Sea and the driver of the day was to build platforms quickly in order to get the oil and revenue streams flowing as soon as possible. The big stick was the fear of 'deferred oil', which was used something like, 'Well we could do that, but if it means we defer oil production by a day that would cost us £x million.'

The technical and logistical challenges were enormous – the North Sea is one of the most inhospitable of regions, with cold waters and 100-foot waves. The oil industry was forced to innovate and adapt to the new environment, pioneering latest technology and leading edge processes. There were spectacular leaps forward as well as catastrophic failures, such as the Alexander Kielland accommodation platform collapse in 1980 and the explosion on the Piper Alpha platform eight years later.

The combination of the environment, the technical challenges and the economic opportunity meant that if you look at the infrastructure that was put into the North Sea you will see that no two platforms are the same, not even two platforms built by a single operator, whether that is BP, Shell or some other company. There are fixed platforms built on steel jackets and others with concrete legs, and here I am talking only of the superficial differences, which in fairness are probably the least important and more justifiable variances. However, if you look at the installed equipment (the pumps, valves, compressors and turbines) then every type of kit and every manufacturer are well represented on most platforms.

Before you ask 'so what?' or come up with some other egalitarian comment about spreading the business around, just let me point out that this means that each platform is weighed down (quite literally) with a profusion of unique spares and manuals for the variety of equipment installed on it, and regularly visited by droves of specialists from each of the manufacturers. Compound this with the cost of buying, transporting and holding all this inventory and multiply it by the life expectancy of the original equipment, and you can start to see a nightmarish total cost of ownership in action. The failure to standardize on selected specifications, equipment and manufacturers has driven huge cost into the industry.

When you are designing an asset that has a life expectancy of more than 30 years the cost of such decisions really can mount up. In this environment, saying 'Yes' to the engineer who wants to 'try this out' or to the buyer who can 'get that at a fantastic price', is amazingly costly. Some operators have been able to justify retrospective rationalization of the equipment on the grounds of reduced people, time and spares – but most just had to live with it all. Others have been very creative in tackling the symptoms, for example identifying the generic or commonly available spares in the long list of original equipment manufacturers' parts list and sourcing them from elsewhere; or commissioning the manufacturer to maintain the equipment and paying for the up-time rather than the asset (very good ideas by the way). All of this is very laudable, but will never equal the total cost of ownership that comes from getting it right first time.

I would like to think I was wide-eyed and naïve when I encountered this in the oil industry, but I cannot make that claim the second time

I came across this on a pan-industry scale. As a management consultant I did some work for a cable company that was in the process of laying fibre cable across the UK to facilitate customer television and telephone services. Once again there was no standardization in any of the assets: all manufacturers were used with a myriad of equipment. In this case the motivator was getting the infrastructure out there as soon as possible and once again it was a sort of Wild West land grab. While you could argue it wasn't as bad as the North Sea – you don't need a helicopter or a supply vessel when you need to repair or maintain something – I would remind you that much of the cable equipment was being put in the ground, under roads and footpaths.

What neither the oil companies nor the cable company were thinking about was the total cost of ownership. They were thinking about the project – design it, build it and pass it to the maintenance department. Total cost of ownership is the cost of the asset throughout the stages of its life, which are shown in Figure 3.1.

Figure 3.1 The stages of the life of an asset

If you calculate total cost of ownership and use this as the basis for figuring out which is the most appropriate solution then you are very likely to make a significant contribution to your organization's profitability over the shorter term and, more important, safeguard it over the longer term. This is because it will force you to think about all aspects of the asset including its design, up-time, maintenance routine, cost of spares and useful life. As a simple example, try running your next photocopier purchase against this model (even one for personal use) and you will soon realize that the most significant factors of the total cost of ownership are the ink cartridges and the necessary paper quality rather than the photocopier machine itself. The same considerations apply to blades for razors, applications for iPhones and batteries for appliances.

Numerous countries have public-private partnerships (PPP). These are typically arrangements between a public sector authority and a private party, in which the private party provides a public service or project and takes responsibility for all financial, technical and operational risk. One good thing about PPP schemes is that they are forcing companies to look more thoroughly at the total cost of ownership because remuneration is on the basis of the services they deliver and not the cost of the construction or operation separately. For example, I was talking to the owner of a new hospital built under a PPP scheme who told me that the traditional lighting provided in operating theatres meant that when bulbs needed to be replaced the operating theatre had to be shut down and specialist engineers and equipment brought in to effect the change. This had huge cost and service implications for the owner, both in respect of downtime and expenditure so, working with the lighting providers, they had invented and installed a new scheme that made the process much simpler and one that took hours rather than days. While the construction cost was higher the running costs were reduced significantly and, because of the PPP structure, when this total cost of ownership optimization opportunity had come to light (couldn't resist the pun – sorry), it made sense to seize it.

I once worked on a project to procure underground storage tanks for petrol stations. When we analysed the total cost of ownership we realized that the biggest costs were associated with digging the original hole and installing the storage tanks, and then reopening the hole, remediating any contamination and replacing the storage tanks if they failed. In this instance the key was to design the tanks so that their useful life expectancy was at least commensurate with the anticipated longevity of the petrol station.

So getting things right first time applies to lots of things. Whether you are setting up a new company, subsidiary or venture, make sure that you think through the consequences of what you are spending your money on. If you are the CEO of something new, make sure that you are focusing on the things that are going to make you famous (hint: it is most likely that this will be something to do with your customer value proposition). If you have to acquire an asset (and I suggest you think long and hard about whether you want to own anything at all) make sure you consider its total cost to your organization and optimize it – right from the start.

Much of the rest of this book covers both current and new opportunities. I thought this was worthy of a chapter of its own because you can only be right first time once.

4 Know your core

Once you have figured out your customer value proposition, you need to construct the supply chain that is best able to deliver it. While doing this you need to decide which activities in the supply chain you are going to do yourself and which you are going to ask other companies to do for you. This in essence is what this chapter is all about.

Before we start it is probably worth laying out some best practices associated with the supply chain that you are going to create. First, in order to be successful it is essential that you are able to articulate your supply chain's value proposition from a position of profound under-standing. Second, you must recognize that you are responsible not only for the customer value proposition but also for the supply chain itself, even if you plan to do nothing more than manage it. This is because both your customers and suppliers believe that it is yours. You and only you can brand, shape and define it. You might take advice on it (indeed I hope you do) but if there is a casting vote – it is yours. The final thing that you must bear in mind is that at some point you are going to delegate responsibility for delivering some components of your supply chain to one or more of your suppliers. The way you do that is going to be fundamental to the success or failure of your supply chain, and is a topic we will come back to.

Now that I have got those points off my chest, let's get back to the nuts and bolts of your supply chain and figure out what you are going to do and what you are going to get someone else to do. To some extent this should be relatively intuitive because it is something that we do in our everyday lives. For example, if you love cleaning (perish the thought) then you are likely to clean your house yourself; if you don't like it or aren't any good at it then you might look for a cleaner. Sometimes, even if you like cleaning, you might decide that you should get a cleaner because the activity is distracting you from something else that is more important, or because you expect to move to a bigger house soon where you cannot possibly do it all by yourself any more. In the world of procurement, what you have just done is assess the activity in the context of both your short- and longer-term requirements and against competing demands.

Another factor in your assessment will be the quality of the supply market, which in this instance will be the availability and costs of good cleaners – for example, if you live in the middle of nowhere then you might not be able to find a cleaner, or you might have to pay more for the service than you are willing to. What we have just done in this simple example is also largely what you would do in business: understand your competence and capacity; assess the current and future importance of the activity; and review the external market and its capability to provide you with what you would consider a good quality and cost-effective service.

Now that we have established the principles, let's see what this means in practice. In this chapter we are going to study the supply chain, review its activities in respect of both your appetite and ability to complete them, and then go on to assess the supply market's capability to undertake any of them for you.

Activities in the supply chain

Over the years I have helped various companies make choices about what they will do in-house and what they will outsource. These 'make versus buy' decisions are easiest if the business defines the candidate activities at the right level, and very difficult and even dangerous if they are either at too high a level or too fragmented. Let me give you an example. Many companies decide to outsource IT which, in my experience, is often a knee-jerk reaction to years of confusion and frustration where the business has faced overruns on project after project without fully understanding why it is happening. Information technology is, to many people and especially those in the boardroom, beyond comprehension. It's a sort of black box that, in their eyes at least, more often than not causes pain. At some point the board members crack and the cry goes up, 'Outsource the lot.' The first mistake has been made and without intervention what the company will end up with is the black box of pain now managed and controlled by a third party. It will still have no better understanding of what IT is all about or what 'good' looks like (particularly for its business) and no idea if it got a good or bad deal from its outsource provider.

This plays into a philosophical debate that has been raging, unresolved, for years around the question: 'Is it best that the owner improves the process and then outsources or should you outsource and let the supplier make the improvements?' On the one hand, if you streamline the process before outsourcing you are keeping the value of those improvements in-house and not handing over the savings to the supplier. On the other hand, the sooner you pass it over to the supplier the sooner you can focus on your core business and the sooner the outsourced business can move to its end state. One way of getting your cake and eating it is to outsource but ensure that under the provisions of the contract you enjoy the cost benefits that are delivered through the supplier's efforts. However, I think this debate is still probably raging unabated because there is actually no one right answer and it is very much horses for courses.

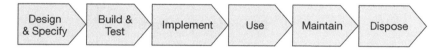

Figure 4.1   Information technology supply chain

However, what I would say is that IT as a single black box should never be outsourced. Instead you need to look at the supply chains that cover IT infrastructure and applications (such as the one illustrated in Figure 4.1) and consider the options of outsourcing for each of the activities on its own merits. This is the sort of analysis that we are going to look at over the next few pages.

Core and non-core

Once you have looked at your supply chain or business process and identified its constituent activities, then it is important, as in the example we looked at for cleaning, to evaluate how well you perform each of the activities currently and assess how important each is to your business. Figure 4.2 provides a framework to support this assessment. The idea is that you assess the activities currently carried out by your organization against two dimensions and plot the results on the matrix. If you assemble a cross-disciplinary team that understands the supply chain under review, this exercise can generate a lot of useful information and analysis. You can also repeat the exercise to differing levels of accuracy. For example you could start with a workshop where you discuss the activities and plot more by knowledgeable gut feel than data. If you decide to take any action as a result of the work, you will probably want to validate the initial view with some more detailed due diligence.

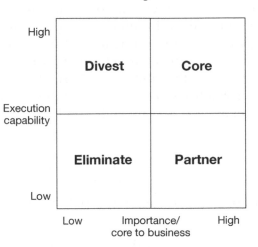

Figure 4.2   Organization capability evaluation matrix

Let me first explain in more detail the two dimensions against which we are going to plot the various activities: execution capability and importance/core to the business.

Execution capability

This is an assessment of how good your company is at performing the activity. This should be evaluated against your current capability, because it is important that the assessment is objective. Obviously the only exception to this would be if there are known changes already under way that will alter your execution capability for better or worse.

It is also important that you have some sort of benchmark against which to assess your organization's capability. These benchmarks need to be identified with care as there is little point in evaluating yourself against a mediocre organization if there are world beaters out there.

Importance/core to the business

Against this dimension you need to evaluate the contribution of each activity to the success of your customer value proposition or business objective. A good way to think about this is to assess what the consequences would be for the business if the activity failed or, with more optimism, what the uplift could be to the business if the activity were executed flawlessly. The sort of questions you are likely to ask yourself will include consideration of the activity's impact upon your profitability, customer proposition, market share, cost base, operational integrity and reputation. Whereas on the first axis it was important to assess current performance, plotting on this axis should be against the activity's future importance to the business, as this could change over time in response to new opportunities, markets or competition.

Within the model, the four quadrants show the strategies you should take for the activities that plot within them. They are eliminate, divest, partner and own.

Eliminate

The extreme response to anything that plots into this quadrant will be that as you aren't very good at the activity and it isn't at all important to your supply chain or company, then the activity should be a candidate for elimination. After all, why do it in the first place if it is non-added value and executed poorly? More realistically, an activity that plots into this quadrant will be something that is of low value to the organization and not executed particularly well. So, while it might not be a candidate for extermination it is one for which you could seek an alternative provider, especially if someone else can do it better than you in terms of quality, cost or time. If you do decide to seek an alternative provider then the business risk is going to be low and therefore your selection criteria for the service provider are likely to be largely ones that would deliver operational excellence and cost-effectiveness to your organization.

Divest

An activity will be plotted into this quadrant if you are very good at it but its outputs are not particularly important to the success of the value proposition. In such a situation you could consider selling off that part of your company, together with its processes and systems, to another entity for which the activity is core. You could even negotiate a deal whereby you sell the business and then buy back the services – it may not be important to you but it is probably still something that you need to have done. What it does mean is that in an environment of scarce resource, you don't need to do it yourself. This type of sale and buy-back construct is one that is particularly popular, especially to smaller organizations that need critical mass, or start-ups that are backed by venture capitalists and keen to kick-start a business around their acquisition. By contracting to become a customer of the entity you are providing an important revenue stream that can have a significant impact on the sale price you receive.

If you look now at the right hand side of the diagram – things that have been plotted in these two quadrants are very important to your business.

Partner

If something is plotted into this quadrant then you are recognizing that you aren't very good at the activity but it is critical to your proposition. In such a situation, it is important to improve your performance and you can do this either alone or with someone to help you. For example, you could invest in the activity – buying skills, processes, tools, systems, etc and really boost your in-house capability. Alternatively, you could look to collaborate with a company that is already very good at doing it. In this scenario you might still want to outsource the activity, but you will want to select your provider very carefully, ensure that you are strategically aligned, incentivize them appropriately and manage them closely – because their success and yours will be inextricably linked.

Core

If an activity is plotted into this quadrant, congratulations are in order. What you are saying here is that the activity is both important to you and something you are already very good at. Therefore I suggest that you will want to do nothing other than continue to invest appropriately in the activity to ensure that you remain in this strong position. After all, the activities in this quadrant are important to your success and they are things that you excel in, and as such you should nurture and relish them.

Once you have plotted things onto this diagram, you will have a clear understanding of what activities you are good at and which ones are important to your success. For activities that plot into three of the four quadrants, you might consider getting suppliers to help you, either through outsourcing, collaboration or sale and buy-back arrangements. I say that you 'might consider' doing this because actually your options are going to be influenced by the capability and willingness of the supply market to help you. There is little point in outsourcing an activity to a third party if it is going to be more expensive and of poorer quality than in-house provision.

Market capability

As we have seen there are many reasons to want to outsource an activity. Two of the more strategic reasons for doing it are that you are not very good at the activity yourself or that the activity is relatively unimportant to your value proposition. Outsourcing it will allow the organization to concentrate on other added-value activities and create capacity, for example by freeing up management time, investment, property, research and development effort and people.

However, the desire to outsource something can only become a reality if there is a supplier capable of taking on the activity for you. Not only that, but ideally the supplier will be able to offer you something extra, something that you couldn't achieve by doing the work in-house. The most obvious of these would be things like lower costs, better quality, greater delivery certainty and reduced risk. In certain circumstances, an organization might be willing to outsource something and receive the same quality service for the same total cost (often to free up capacity to concentrate resources on more important matters), but I have rarely seen an organization willing to pay a premium to receive that which it used to do just as well in-house. Consequently, the deciding factors are likely to be the quality and compatibility of the supply market. I would like to introduce Figure 4.3 to help with this market analysis. Once again I will start by describing the two dimensions against which to assess the suppliers and the supply market.

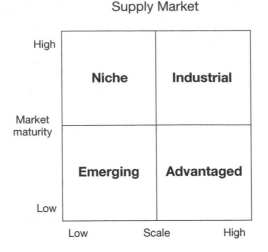

Figure 4.3 Supply market capability evaluation matrix

Market maturity

Market maturity is a combination of many things including longevity, stability and strategies. For example, suppliers and customers in the world of business process outsourcing (BPO) have been around for decades. The market is well established and could be considered very mature. Other examples of mature markets would be in IT infra-structure such as data centre outsourcing, and in property such as facilities management and maintenance services. At the opposite extreme would be knowledge services outsourcing (KSO), which seeks to take on added-value activities that historically might have been provided by consultancy companies or legal firms (eg providing market analysis to facilitate strategic decisions and constructing large contracts).

Scale

This dimension considers the scale of the market and particularly the number and size of the suppliers within it. For example, IT infra-structure providers operate on a large scale with broad geographic presence whereas a legal firm that provides conveyancing services to a mortgage underwriter is unlikely to expand beyond its domestic market or legislative environment.

The quadrants provide the assessment of the market; they are as follows.

Emerging

Both the market and its suppliers are currently immature. Some companies are already established but are relatively small. To survive they are likely to want to grow either vertically or horizontally, possibly by acquisition – this adds uncertainty to the prospects for companies in this quadrant. You may consider outsourcing to one of the companies but not for business-critical services and probably only if there is something in it for you (eg recognition as a cornerstone customer with preferential arrangements or shareholding). An example of this type of company would be one that delivers cloud computing services; despite the fact that large companies such as IBM are in this business the expertise and scale is slight. This will obviously change over time, which is why this quadrant is the most dynamic.

Niche

Some markets are very mature yet the players in them can still be niche. This would happen where economies of scale are not available despite the market's longevity, and is likely to occur when services need to be tailored to meet specific requirements. This market is unlikely to be commoditized as the services delivered are individual to the client. The client is likely to be attracted by suppliers who have deep technical expertise, possibly offering leverage and scale in a declining market. By way of an example: in banking, as customers move to electronic forms of payment, the demand for cheque processing and clearing is declining steadily (though will remain for several years yet) and the service is technically complex and business critical. Several years ago, to overcome these issues, Unisys, Barclays, HSBC and Lloyds Banking Group created a BPO joint venture in the UK called iPSL. This venture would plot into this quadrant as it is highly skilled, complex and limited in scale.

Advantaged

The market is immature but the companies that operate in it have already acquired scale and are recognized leaders. Companies in this quadrant are likely to be operating in areas that lend themselves to scale either through process efficiency or the use of automation. As the market matures, it could still offer opportunities for growth, but the companies are already cost advantaged. Growth is more likely to come through new geographies or expanded service offerings. The benefits on offer from these suppliers (in terms of scale and investment) will encourage you to consider contracting with a supplier in this quadrant for even your most critical applications. You will want to enjoy economies of scale and might want a contract that allows you to share in the benefits as the market matures. For example, suppliers in this quadrant might have at their disposal levers of value (such as technology platforms that can be shared across clients) that are as yet unexploited because of the immaturity of the market.

Industrial

Suppliers in this quadrant will be world-class service providers that have grown to scale in a mature market. Companies that provide IT infrastructure and software development services such as IBM, Accenture, TATA and Wipro are obvious examples. Other suppliers might be contract manufacturers in the pharmaceutical industry or payroll service providers.

This tool helps you to assess the supply market's maturity and its capability to operate at scale. Not even the combination of immaturity and lack of scale need be a show-stopper as the supplier's positioning must be seen in the context of your requirements. However, it will influence your outsourcing strategy. For example, if the activity isn't particularly core to you, you might be happy to become a cornerstone customer to one of the emerging suppliers, effectively allowing the supplier to use your requirements, volume and existing capability to grow its service offer. This can be commercially attractive, with options ranging from low-cost service provision to shareholding. Similarly some niche suppliers will never achieve substantial scale, even in a mature market, but have expertise that is valued and needed by the client for its more critical requirements.

At other times the scale of the suppliers might influence your decision making, as it is important that you can find at least one supplier to which your volume is important but not crucial. If your requirements are low volume, a small or medium-sized supplier might best meet your needs as your requirements may not be attractive to an industrial-strength player. Conversely, if your requirements are significant then you probably need a supplier or two that can readily absorb your volume and still have two-thirds of their business from other customers.

In summary, the positioning and options are relative to your scale and requirements and therefore both elements need to be considered in conjunction with each other.

The models in action

Years ago I outsourced a warehouse and logistics operation for an oil company. The warehouse operation itself was something of a sleepy hollow and had been rather neglected for some time. The facility was used to hold and manage the owned inventory for a large fleet of oil and gas supertankers and act as a collection point for other materials and spares before they were bundled up and freighted to rendezvous with the various tankers as they sailed the oceans of the world.

The problem of the neglected warehouse was identical to that experienced by most activities that are not seen as core to the business. Despite the warehouse staff's best intentions (and even the best intentioned can only remain enthusiastic for a certain time in such an environment), execution had slipped from good to poor and, with no investment in its methods, equipment and capabilities, the whole operation had become outdated. This meant that by the time I came along, the only viable option was to outsource. I embarked on this with gusto as I firmly believed that if I could pick the right company to outsource to then I would improve the service and at the same time give the people in the operation the opportunity to move to a company that would value their skills as core to its business and therefore nurture both the people and the operation. My ambition was to deliver a real win-win-win for the warehouse staff, the fleet and the acquirer.

The warehouse wasn't important in its own right as it provided little more than a storage facility and collection point for materials. However, the warehousing and logistics operation together supported the maintenance and repair operation for a fleet of oil and gas supertankers, so the operation was business critical to the fleet because it held, consolidated and delivered vital equipment to the vessels, and the mail and billet doux to their crews, finding them in port anywhere around the world. The logistics was already outsourced albeit in a piecemeal fashion to a rather under-scale company and, as mentioned, the warehouse was dusty to say the least.

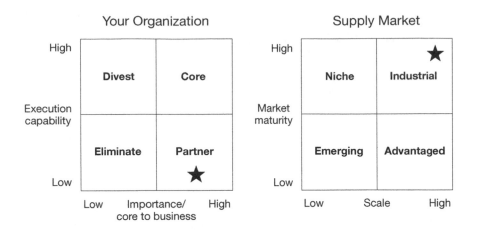

Figure 4.4 Warehouse outsourcing example

The logistics market was mature and there were several global suppliers capable of supporting our needs. One of the challenges we faced was making our requirements significant enough to be important to one of these large suppliers. To do this we expanded the scope of our requirements to include the inbound logistics operations (from the parts manufacturers and suppliers to the warehouse). This increased the attractiveness of our business to our provider as there was a significant increase in its revenue opportunity in an area that was its bread-and-butter activity and a real sweet spot. An additional benefit of this to the oil company was that the logistics provider would have sole accountability for the end-to-end operation – from factory gate to supertanker.

The oil company picked a good supplier and incentivized its performance through the terms of the contract and a gainshare agreement. It retained ownership of the warehouse and leased it to the new supplier. The warehouse staff transferred to the supplier and became core to their new employer, and overall the costs of the operation were slashed as waste was eliminated.

This appears to be a relatively simple example, so let's up the ante. The oil company only needed the warehousing and logistics operation because it had to transport oil and gas around the world in supertankers. As the product is being transported its value can soar or plummet depending upon the market. It can be bought and sold many times over while on the high seas and therefore reliable and cost-effective pick-up and delivery are essential. What would have happened if I had screwed up the logistics operation and as a result one of the supertankers had broken down? Let's talk consequences and what I like to refer to as 'consequential supply chains'.

Consequential supply chains

A word of warning before we start: everything has consequences and if we aren't careful this could be a brilliant excuse for inaction. This is not what I am advocating. Instead, my premise is that if we look at the bigger picture before we start then we can take into account the core operations and ensure they are safeguarded. Let's look again at supply chains.

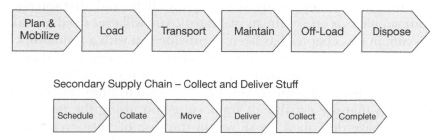

Figure 4.5 Consequential supply chain study for oil and gas

In Figure 4.5 we can see the primary supply chain – the objective of which is to collect and deliver oil and gas to various time, quality, safety and cost parameters. The secondary supply chain is to drop off to, and pick up goods and equipment from, a vessel in port. The cost of the primary supply chain is probably hundreds of millions and its opportunity to contribute to the reputation and profitability of the company is high. If I do a great job optimizing the secondary supply chain in isolation (eg only meeting vessels when they pass through Singapore), I could really screw up the primary supply chain (eg the crew down tools because there is no mail; the vessel breaks down on the high sea and cannot be repaired; or the crew's productivity is limited because there is no maintenance to do on a leg of a voyage as the spares aren't on board). Beyond losing my job, the consequences are significant because I wouldn't have thought them through.

Luckily this didn't happen, but unfortunately this sort of thing does happen every day: the high-tech equipment sea freighted from China that is obsolete before it arrives; the cash machine that runs out of money because it can't hold enough to meet regular demand; or the brand damage caused by using unsustainable or unethical sources of supply.

The challenge is to understand enough about the primary supply chain to optimize the secondary supply chain in the context of its ambition. Once you know the parameters, you can be pretty radical in your optimization of the secondary supply chain and know that you will at worst be doing no harm to the primary, and potentially adding huge value to both.

In summary

The decision about what you as a company will do and what you ask of your suppliers is one of the most strategic you will ever need to make. My aim in this chapter has been to provide you with a framework to analyse the activities in your supply chain and categorize them in various ways. Once you have evaluated you own capability and your appetite to undertake an activity then you need to study the potential suppliers that are capable of supporting you, using the two frameworks I have described. As shown in the case of outsourcing warehousing, part of the dynamic is to find appropriate suppliers and make your business attractive to them. Taking the time to study all the sourcing options available to you is time well spent in shaping the future success of you organization.

5 Handling the complexity

In the first chapter I mentioned that no company was an island and introduced the idea of supply chains and how the success of any business venture hinges on how well the owner of the supply chain can harness the capabilities of both his or her organization and its key suppliers to deliver the value proposition and delight its customers. In this chapter I want to explore this interconnected world in much more detail and provide some hints and tips on how best to manage it.

Anyone who has ever watched starlings flocking at sunset can't have failed to be amazed at how beautiful, harmonious and complicated their movements are. The flocks can comprise hundreds if not thousands of birds, and these creatures are not considered to be particularly intelligent (no offence intended). Despite this I have never seen two birds crash into one another, indeed the most discordance I have ever seen is the odd one flapping its wings madly to catch up with the rest. There has been copious research into how these birds can achieve such cohesion, and what is interesting is that flocking behaviour can be simulated using three simple rules: separation (avoid getting too close to its neighbour); alignment (fly in the same direction as its neighbours) and cohesion (steer towards the average position of its neighbours). Studies have upheld these rules as accurate in the real world.

The rules that apparently harmonize the collective behaviour of birds, ants, bees and fish have been used to create agent-based systems that in turn have been applied to predict complex business situations (Bonabeau and Meyer, 2001). For example, the study of ants and their pheromone trails has been used to improve the routing of packages of data across telecommunication networks, and other models have been used to successfully predict the impact on the NASDAQ of changes to things such as the tick rate.

I was lucky enough to be involved on the periphery of this when as a consultant with Ernst & Young I worked with the BiosGroup (co-founded by Stuart Kauffman and Ernst & Young) to use these agent-based systems to develop the model for complex downstream oil distribution networks in the United States. I mention this because I think it illustrates that even the most complicated of interactions, involving hundreds of autonomous decision makers, can be modelled and forecast provided you can understand the motivations and objectives of the individuals involved.

Supply chains across organizations

So now let's now move on from starlings to look at how businesses organize themselves. Supply chains involve multiple disparate entities, and if you think about a supply chain as I have explained it so far, you can see that it is a series of activities carried out across different organizational entities where each produces a deliverable that is passed to the next entity and so on until finally the completed product or service is delivered to the customer. These 'organizational entities' can be your suppliers and their suppliers, but they can also be the different departments within your company. These internal departments can typically be defined as functions, product lines or business units.

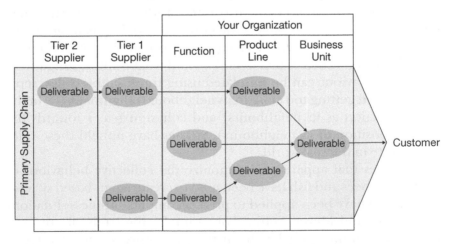

Figure 5.1   Supply chains flow across organizations

Figure 5.1 illustrates the complexity of these interactions. The challenge this complexity presents and the ways in which it can be overcome are the subjects that I will tackle in this chapter. Before we start exploring that, let's look at some of the entities depicted in the diagram, starting with those that are within the organization.

Functions

Functions are a great way of enabling centres of excellence and creating talent pools that the company can draw on and to which individuals feel a sense of belonging. Functions are typically organizational entities like marketing, operations, IT, HR and so on. Many organizations have outsourced some of these functions either in whole or in part. The attraction is that functions are self-contained units with clear management structures. The challenge is that the services of these functions are utilized by other parts of the organization in support of their supply chains, meaning that outsourcing along functional lines can inhibit the subsequent optimization of the supply chains and the other processes that they support.

One multinational found, after applying functional outsourcing, that it could not achieve transformational change because it had too many stakeholders and third parties involved, each of which had little vested interest in re-engineering. After much deliberation the multinational was forced to bring back in-house the work that it had outsourced, transform along supply chain lines and then later outsource to new vendors with new scopes of work and service levels. This is an extreme example but not uncommon. It can be difficult enough to get your own organization to operate in the best way to support your supply chains; when activities are undertaken for you by a variety of third parties, each of which has competing priorities, your attempts at radical re-engineering or transformation that also threaten their revenue streams can become almost impossible.

You might at this point be wondering why this is so important. It is because functions do not just support one supply chain or process within your organization: rather they support many, often with competing priorities and objectives. Therefore getting a function, whether owned or outsourced, to support a particular supply chain can be more complex than a single-point solution between a supplier and a supply chain.

Product lines

In most companies part of the business will be organized along product lines. These are specialist units focused on producing products or services. Even consultancies that are purely people organizations will typically be split into product/service lines and customer-facing units.

Business units

A business unit is a customer-focused part of the organization that is responsible for selling its product or service to the customer. As such, most customer-oriented companies give accountability for the delivery of the customer value proposition to the business unit. Units are typically aligned to the market segments to which they market and sell the company's product or services.

Supplier tiers and tears

Suppliers can deliver directly to functions, product lines and business units within your organization. Furthermore your suppliers will more than likely have their own suppliers that are supplying components that will be contributing to the supply chain. Therefore the third parties associated with the supply chain are also interrelated and can be structured logically into various tiers. A tier one supplier is one that has a contractual relationship with the owner of the supply chain, and a tier two supplier will have a contractual relationship with the tier one supplier (as shown in Figure 5.1). For example, an automotive manufacturer could have a contractual relationship with a tier one supplier for the provision of an anti-lock braking system (ABS) and that supplier will have contractual relationships with other suppliers for the delivery of the various components of the ABS.

Tier one suppliers therefore are often responsible for the delivery of a service or a system and in support of this their tier two suppliers will provide tier one with a variety of components. The relationships between the supply chain owner and the tiers of suppliers can be both beneficial and detrimental and as such either a huge source of value or of frustration. When I worked in the oil industry a lot of the big construction projects were subcontracted to service companies such as Halliburton, KBR and Schlumberger. The operators (Shell,

BP, etc) would run huge sourcing exercises to select the most appropriate subcontractor for a particular project. In responding to the tender, the service companies would, in turn, run huge sourcing exercises with their supplier shortlists, and this would repeat down the tiers of supply. At some point these shortlists would converge and tier two and three suppliers would end up receiving tender invitations (all slightly different) from four or five different sources for the provision of the same good or service. It doesn't take a genius (thank goodness) to figure out that this process created a huge burden and cost both to the suppliers and ultimately for the supply chain owner (after all, someone has to pay for it).

This takes me nicely to my next hobby horse in respect of supplier tiers – laying off risk. Oil is an expensive, complex and physically dirty business with huge opportunities and significant risks. What a lot of supply chain owners like to do is lay off risk to their service providers, which in turn cascaded the risk into their supply base. Ultimately this risk (a premium for which will have been added each time it is laid off) is going to rest with a two-bit company that has no assets and is quite happy to say 'Yes' to the risk and go bankrupt if that risk materializes. The extreme outcome of this is that the supply chain owner, by laying off the risk, has achieved nothing but increased cost.

Enough of this negative frame of mind – let me put on my happy hat and talk now about all the good things supplier tiers can bring. By assigning a first-tier supplier, the client can harness its significant knowledge and experience to bring together the best combination of suppliers to deliver what is required. The expert supplier bringing together a group of other suppliers to deliver the required systems or services (as opposed to the components or activities that would be delivered by individual suppliers) can make an enormous contribution to the supply chain.

For example, in the last chapter we discussed consequential supply chains and the fact that the organization must optimize its secondary supply chains in the context of the primary supply chain to safeguard the overall value proposition. In the automotive example, the ABS will be a secondary supply chain and the primary supply chain will be the vehicle being manufactured. Optimizing the secondary supply chain in such a way that it adds value to the vehicle manufacture could add significant 'consequential' value.

These supplier groupings can also work together for a variety of clients, thereby transferring and honing knowledge over time. Similarly a client can encourage a coalition of the suppliers it believes are most likely to meet its needs rather than rely on historic relationships or chance.

Marching to the same beat

Let's recap: we have a primary supply chain and lots of secondary supply chains. The activities in these supply chains will be undertaken by a variety of in-house functions and business units and by third parties. The third parties themselves are organized into various tiers and, other than with the tier one suppliers, the supply chain owner doesn't have a formal (contractual) relationship with any of them. When you bring all this together it can look overwhelming and the challenge is obvious: how on earth can the owner of the supply chain make sure that all these moving parts work together to delight the organization's customers? My answer is that you can do this more easily than you might think and the silver bullets, if there are any, are labelled 'functional requirements' and 'outcome specifications'.

Functional requirements

Clients have a responsibility to specify what they need and they should do so with a great deal of precision. If it is for a piece of equipment, they might want to specify its capabilities, dimensions and characteristics. If it is for a service, they will want to define what 'good' looks like in respect of quality, output and timeliness. These are all functional specifications – because what the client is doing is specifying what the good or services should be capable of delivering. What the clients are not doing is specifying how the supplier goes about satisfying the requirement. The client wants cold air, not necessarily that air conditioner, or personal computing, not necessarily that laptop. Functional requirements help the supplier to understand what the client needs and values – they do not constrain the supplier in respect of applying its expertise to meet that need. In this way they provide the directions that will help to create the desired result.

Outcome specifications

In Chapter 2, we recognized that the key to any organization's success is a clear understanding of what its customers value now and in the future about the good or service they buy. We also exposed the danger of mixing up what customers value with what your company is good at delivering. Success requires that you clearly articulate your customer value proposition and use that as a rallying crying for your organization and its suppliers.

Outcome specifications are an extension of this and can be used to draw together disparate stakeholders and suppliers to deliver what your supply chain needs. I remember someone complaining to me years ago that a design engineering firm had not delivered what he had asked for. Apparently he wanted a simple design made of standard components and what he received was a complex design with a plethora of bespoke features. I suggested to my friend that if he had wanted something simple he should have clearly specified the outcome he required and offered a fixed price for the work and not paid for time and materials.

This can happen a lot. Less than 10 years ago, advertising agencies were remunerated in the form of sizeable commissions payable against the customer's media spending and production costs. This meant that the more the ad agency spent on its customer's behalf the more it earned. Proctor & Gamble pioneered a different reward structure and caused a furore when it decided to tie the agency's remuneration to the campaign's impact on global brand sales. P&G did this because, as its Director of Public Affairs and Media, Gary Cunningham, acknowledged, 'companies advertise to sell more products' (Curtis, 2000). What he had specified was his desired *outcome specification.*

While this example is almost 10 years old, it is interesting that by 2007 this type of payment by results (PBR) reward mechanism is still only used by slightly over half of all customers of marketing-related services. The approach to advertising by Proctor & Gamble is a great example of an outcome specification – understanding what you will value from the service you receive and using that to specify your functional requirements and shape the reward structures.

Focusing on outcomes also helps the client to transfer responsibility for the design of the solution to the supplier, which should be much more capable of figuring out how best to deliver the desired outcome than the client. Which takes me to another of the truisms of good procurement: that the customer knows best what he or she needs and the right supplier knows best how to satisfy that need.

There will of course be a variety of outcome specifications associated with even the simplest of supply chains and the challenge is to ensure that they are compatible both upward and downward. A good outcome specification will detail all the elements that will define success to its requester (whether that be the supply chain owner, business unit, product line, function or tier one or two supplier). It will contain the measure of success and enabling criteria. For example, the outcome specification for P&G could be something like: 'To improve our brand recognition by 5 per cent in our key markets by the end of 2011 while reducing our total advertising expenditure by 5 per cent above market norm.' This should then be enshrined in the contract and drive the financial reward structure as well as the service levels. When the media agency then contracts with its suppliers, the outcome and functional specification for the goods and services being supplied should be compatible with this broader ambition. Using outcome and functional specifications in this way helps all the moving parts of the supply chain to remain focused on the same goals while obviously their contribution to the success will vary dependent upon their capability and role.

In summary

There are likely to be various organizations involved in delivering your customer value propositions. More than likely there will tiers of suppliers external to your company, each with their own goals and objectives, culture and values. There will also be different units within your own organization, each with its own specialist skills and ambitions. You can't combine these organizations in order to deliver your customer value proposition but you can align them. Like starlings flocking in the sky they remain individual entities but need to operate homogeneously by following some basic rules. Your primary weapons for aligning all these disparate elements will be the outcome and functional specifications. By knowing what it is that your customer values and translating this into clear requirements for each entity, you establish the framework under which they will flock harmoniously to deliver it.

6 What's the issue? We can all do procurement

I really want to agree with this statement! By now, you probably feel that procurement is too important to be left with the procurement department, and you are absolutely right. As soon as you bought into the concept of core versus non-core, you moved procurement centre stage in the attainment of your company's business strategy. However, you probably didn't notice this and probably neither did your procurement department.

Procurement isn't order-taking or even order-placing any more: it is a key business competence. Effective supplier management isn't just a hygiene factor; instead it is about excellence and flawless delivery of your customer value proposition.

So, if procurement is a strategic competence in your organization, who is going to do it? You could look to your corporate strategy team, or what about R&D, the marketers, the procurement department, the design engineers, the logistics providers, the sales force? The answer is of course, 'Yes' to all the above: what you really need is a cross-disciplinary team. The answer lies in your supply chain and the disciplines involved in it; see Figure 6.1.

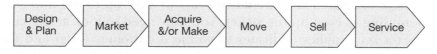

Figure 6.1 Cross-disciplinary supply chain

To optimize your supply chain you need to involve the people who play a part in all aspects of it. That means the engineers who design the product, the marketers who develop the advertising campaign, the plant managers who manufacture it, etc. If you have outsourced some of the activities you will also at some point need to involve your suppliers.

In this chapter we will explore the role of the organization in good procurement, the role of the procurement department in good procurement, the value of a cross-disciplinary team and the importance of recognizing and valuing the contribution of each discipline in the process. We will also look at the role of the board in helping to get this right.

We all love to buy

Everyone loves to buy and it's not just about getting something that we have been yearning for: we love the whole process of buying. We love thinking about something new. We like the sales people who enthusiastically tell us how our lives will be transformed and describe the features that we hadn't even considered but soon become convinced that they will become essential to our well-being. We like the break in the routine of our day job and we love the fact that it is our decision to make and that the fawning sales person knows it. There is very little difference in the levels of enjoyment between whether we are spending our own money or our company's money – other than that the scale of the company's spending is likely to be much different to our own.

Suppliers have always known this fundamental truth and for years have designed their sales structure to exploit it. Thousands of hours are spent every year by suppliers' sales staff trying to figure out your company: identifying the decision makers, understanding the politics, managing the key stakeholders and closing the sale. I certainly know that a good way to find out what is happening in my own organization is to ask a well-connected supplier.

Client organizations have taken years to wake up to this and start attempting to even up the stakes. You only need to look at the sales effort a key supplier dedicates to you as a customer (lots) and the resources you as a customer dedicate to managing it as a supplier (less) to know this is true. Evening up the stakes doesn't start with getting more people involved in managing the supplier (this comes later); instead it starts with management information and coordination. What you need to do is start asking and answering questions.

Who do you spend your money with? Which departments are spending the money? What are you buying and are you getting value for money?

Deserve the suppliers you need

A good test of the maturity of the client organization's management of its suppliers is to look at the account teams that the suppliers deploy. When the account team come in to see you, ask yourself how much of the time is spent discussing the value you are getting from the things you have already bought and how much time is spent on what they want to sell to you next. In my experience, encouraging the supplier to focus on the former often means that it has to change the composition of its team to include operational delivery people – which is a great first step. If it is any consolation, the most gullible buyers are usually the most successful sales people!

One of the key ways a supplier manages its customers is to divide and conquer. The more avenues a supplier has into the organization the more it understands what is going on and the more it safeguards its revenue stream. This is achieved in several ways: the client never gets an holistic view of its spend with the supplier and therefore the relationship stays below the radar and isn't scrutinized; when a relationship sours in one part of the organization, others continue to flourish unaffected; if there is a dispute in one part of the organization, the supplier's exposure is likely to be the revenue associated with that particular relationship and not the whole shebang.

You are probably wondering at this huge change of tack: for several chapters I have been banging on about the importance of suppliers to your success and now I am having a dig at them. This couldn't be further from the truth – what I am trying to say is that a customer gets the suppliers it deserves and the first thing you need to do is to deserve the suppliers you need. Getting to bedrock in a client/supplier relationship is vital to ensuring that your strategic alliances are not built on shifting sand. Once you have hit bedrock, you can build lasting and mutually beneficial relationships – not before. Sometimes this requires you to excavate away years of mismanagement, over-pricing, under-performance and unequal relationships.

This means that your organization (and I am using this word advisedly as I don't mean a bit of it, I mean the whole) needs to get its act together. You need to manage the suppliers holistically – whether this is across departments or geographies – and this must start with knowing as much about your relationships with them as they know about their relationships with you.

This discipline has to start at the top. I don't think as many deals are done on the golf course as they used to be (though I do play golf just in case) but it is true that getting the attention of a CEO or board member is worth its weight in gold to a supplier – whatever its agenda. If there is a procurement policy about how the procurement process is conducted across the company, it has to be complied with across the whole company and not just by the rest of us. I have worked in too many consensus-oriented companies to think that getting the buy-in of the CEO and the board is the panacea for all ills, but getting them on side for good procurement is an essential first step in most of them.

The buy-in of your CEO works for your external stakeholders too – never underestimate the power of an on-message statement delivered to a supplier by the CEO. For one, it shows the supplier that the organization has its act together when a supplier hears the same message from the bottom to the top of the tree. The 'CEO's attention' is probably an as yet undocumented law of physics – I for one subscribe to the adage: what interests my boss fascinates me.

So you have the boss interested; what's next? I always think the biggest challenge to ensuring an organization marches to its own drumbeat is the middle layer of the organization – the layer that is empowered but doesn't always see the big picture. Key to this layer is finding something that is important to them in what you are espousing. An appeal to support the 'greater good' doesn't always cut it when you are faced with busy executives struggling to achieve their business plans, and even if they buy into the principle it won't get high up on their agenda unless it contributes to it.

Another reason why you need everyone singing from the same hymn sheet is that you need to be capable of delivering on your promises and your threats. When you strike a great deal with your suppliers, part of the reason for their pricing will have been an expectation of volume. Now you need to deliver that volume. Conversely, if you remove business from a supplier then that business has to dry up.

Maverick buying behaviour is a canker to good procurement and needs a mixture of carrots and sticks to wipe out. The carrots mean that you need to make the right way the easiest way for everyone. You need to provide readily available pan-organization, supplier-related information to the person who is meeting the supplier's sales team and promote the use of preferred suppliers through easy-to-use purchasing systems. The sticks are compliance management reports, objectives on your performance management framework and disciplinary processes. The balance between the two will be driven by your corporate culture. The IBMs of the world operate a 'three strikes and you are out' approach to procurement disciplines, while the BPs let a thousand flowers bloom. Picking the right line is pretty important to the overall success of your campaign.

This is where procurement proficiency comes into its own. I have never seen a procurement department that is more than a fraction of 1 per cent of the total size of the organization. You can have the best procurement department in the world and it can never have the impact on the organization's performance that a procurement-proficient workforce can have. And the big question is, do you want a bow tie or a diamond?

Bow ties and diamonds

I think we would all agree that we want to present a united front to our suppliers; we want to make sure they don't divide and conquer us and we want to have as much knowledge of their business with us as they have. There are two ways of achieving this: restricted access or informed access.

A company can decide that there will be a limited number of named contacts in its organization interfacing with a limited number of named contacts in the supplier organization. This will ensure that the interface between the two organizations is disciplined and any deals are executed in line with company policy. Figure 6.2 (our bow tie) illustrates this relationship. It is unlikely to be as pointed as the diagram depicts as in reality there will be a variety of nominated contacts in both client and supplier organizations.

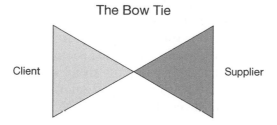

Figure 6.2 The bow tie client-supplier relationship

The downside of the restricted relationship is that ad hoc contacts will be curtailed and that all information between client and supplier is in effect filtered through the named conduits. This can work for some relationships, those that are not strategic or business important for instance, as it removes the noise from what is a commodity transaction. At the extreme of this relationship one could imagine that the conduit is some sort of electronic link between systems.

Now let's look at the diamond, in Figure 6.3. The premise of the informed relationship is that contact is varied and vast. This model works best for strategic relationships where the success of the two organizations is linked in some way and the measure of success is more than just commercial.

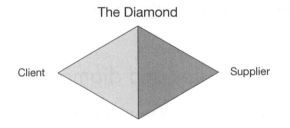

Figure 6.3   The diamond client-supplier relationship

To be successful, participants of the informed relationship must be just that: informed. They need to understand all aspects of the relationship that exists between the two organizations. This works better on a pull rather than push model, by which I mean that the information should be available as required (pulled) rather than pushed out to the people involved in the relationship. This is because all these touch points are likely to be for different purposes and durations and therefore information must be pertinent and timely.

The people involved in this relationships model must be procurement savvy. They must know what they should and should not discuss with the supplier and when (eg no commercial conversations if a tender is under way), their company's procurement policy (eg what the thresholds are for involving the procurement department in the deal), to always use their company's standard terms of business and not the suppliers', and to never pay again for something that is already provisioned in the contract.

The role of the procurement department

If you look at your direct costs you will probably find that you spend as much with your suppliers as you do on your staff. There are some organizations that are either more outsourced or more in-sourced – but as a rule of thumb this will be in the right ballpark. Now look at your HR department and it is probably much larger than your procurement department – yet your HR department is all about getting people who are inside your organization and who share your reward and value structure to do the right thing over a long period of time. Your procurement department on the other hand is about getting suppliers (aka people) who belong to other organizations with different and sometimes conflicting reward and value structures to do the right thing over a long period of time. Key in both functions is selecting and attracting the right people in the first place and rewarding the behaviours you value.

I am sure that last paragraph incensed quite a few of you – especially when I mentioned the responsibility of the HR department. You are thinking that HR, though it has a valuable role to play, is not responsible for selecting talent nor is it responsible for performance management of individuals, nor their training and development – you are. You are the line manager and you know what skills you need now and in the future. You use professional help (your HR team) to help understand the personnel market and what it takes to attract the right talent; to provide the structure of performance management and talent development and to ensure you comply with legislation and regulations.

Now let's translate that to the world of procurement. In my experience there are two models for involving the procurement department. There are the organizations that ignore the procurement team until everything is decided and they need either a contract set up or some help in getting out of one that was ill-judged. Then there are the organizations that involve procurement from the get-go. You will not need a crystal ball to realize that I subscribe to the second of these models. What you should also realize is that this model is not suggesting, even for a nanosecond, that the procurement department is the decision maker. What I am suggesting is that it is used in the same way you use HR. Like HR, the procurement department has a vital role to play as part of the team: the cross-functional team.

In summary

This chapter has been all about getting you organization match-fit to deserve the suppliers it needs. Suppliers invest a great deal of time and effort in getting to know your organization. If you leave them to it, you will get what they want you to have, on their terms, and not what you need on your own terms. Complex organizations have complex relationships with their most important suppliers. Many people within both organizations talk to each other on a regular basis and do deals in isolation of each other. Only by garnering all the participants in the relationship, and that means everybody from the top of your organization down, and by coordinating their interactions with the supplier holistically to make sure that each deal is achieving your organization's goals, will you get your suppliers to dance to your tune.

7 Executive sponsorship and priorities

If, as I hope is the case, you are starting to think that your company could reap rewards from better management of its third-party expenditure then this chapter is pretty critical to the success of the next stage in our journey. This chapter is all about the importance of your sponsorship and direction setting.

I touched upon executive sponsorship in the last chapter and will now expand on it some more in this. What I want to start to explore is what your priorities are going to be for your procurement-proficient organization. Setting your priorities is a bit like fixing a compass. Improved procurement can deliver lots of different things to the organization and only you as one of its leaders can figure out what is most important and when.

Fixing the compass

So first of all you probably need to figure out what would deliver most value to your organization and the best thing to look at is its strategic imperatives.

If you need to improve profitability quickly then there are few better places to start than on your external expenditure. It is nearly always much easier, less costly and more immediate to change your supply arrangements than it is to reduce your staff size. I will go into much more detail about this in Chapter 13.

You might be going through a merger or acquisition. What I have just mentioned holds good here too. The bigger cost reduction opportunities are going to come from rationalizing your IT, your property footprint and your operating model, but they will come further down the line and will require considerable investment. The power house that will deliver the synergies you promised to your investors in the first year or 18 months will be procurement: moving volume to the best contracts, leveraging your new-found scale and simply turning off duplicate spend (for example you aren't going to need two sets of audit fees or all those insurance premiums). Obviously procurement will also play a key role in your merger or acquisition over time as you start to streamline and re-engineer supply chains, decide whether you are going to in-source or outsource key activities, design your target operating model and generally implement the to-be organization.

On the other hand, you might be most worried about supply continuity, especially in uncertain economic times when your key suppliers might be vulnerable. You need to look no further than the upheaval of 2008–2010 and its attendant credit crunch to know that even the most invulnerable of companies suddenly looked shaky, and if these companies supply something that is critical to you then it is well worth focusing some attention on this. Managing supply continuity will require you to mobilize not only your procurement people but also finance and risk departments, and those involved in managing the suppliers. There are lots of lag indicators obviously, but the most important ones to supply continuity are the leading indicators, those signs of stress such as early payment requests, disappearing staff, hunger for additional work with clear revenue streams attached, and a reluctance to go the extra mile without visible and tangible reward.

Alternatively your priority might be to grow revenues: through developing new customer propositions; introducing or evolving products; growing market share; or entering new territories. In this case the right focus for your procurement efforts is likely to be on your supply chains and the selection and management of your key suppliers. You might want to run supply chain innovation or collaboration workshops where you and your key suppliers share ambitions and capabilities in order to identify opportunities for you to develop deeper and broader relationships for mutual gain.

You will see, even from this short list, that each strategic ambition will require a somewhat different approach to the management of your third-party spend and key suppliers. Each will also require the mobilization of different stakeholders within and outside your organization that are appropriately incentivized to deliver specific objectives.

What this should make clear is that it is vital that setting the procurement priorities for your organization is a job that has to be done by you and your board. Leaving direction setting to your middle managers, or worse still your procurement department, will not deliver you the outcome that you need. There are lots of reasons for this but the key one is once again that procurement might not be rocket science but it is very difficult to do well. Wherever procurement sits within your organization there will be lots of competing voices both for its attention and its priorities. Without board-level attention, direction setting and support then procurement is unlikely to fulfil its promise in your organization.

Your sponsorship

While Jean-Luc Picard from 'Star Trek' may not be the leader you are, he did have a great and meaningful punch line that is very relevant to any business: after determining a course of action he adds, 'Make it so.' This type of sponsorship, your sponsorship, is important regardless of the sort of organization you run or its culture.

Obviously if you are in a centralized organization where decisions are made at the top and then implemented without question, your identification of and overt sponsorship of your procurement agenda are critical. If you haven't endorsed the agenda, it will not happen. What is less well recognized is that if you are in a more laissez-faire organization, procurement effectiveness is likely to be a pipedream without your executive-level endorsement. This is because good procurement is tough. It is tough because there are lots of moving parts.

First of all there is your 'organization' – don't be fooled by this single, rather misleading word, which implies order and cohesion. Your organization comprises people who sell, who deliver and who support, and they may well be organized like this in various departments and functions. These departments are likely to have many objectives in common but they will also have some that are different. The juxtaposition of these objectives and their relative priority within your organization is going to determine success or failure. There is a wonderful story of John F Kennedy visiting NASA at the height of the space race. He encountered a man sweeping the floor and asked him what his job was. 'I'm putting a man on the Moon, Mr President,' the janitor replied. Not many organizations have the luxury of such clarity but those that do have it because the leaders of their organization have it and have clearly communicated this understanding to all those who work with them.

Second, there are your suppliers and as we have already discovered they are probably better connected across your organization than many of your employees. Just ask yourself how many of your employees have the same level of access to your diary as some of your suppliers – especially those from the major consultancy and accountancy firms. Furthermore, suppliers are rather like an iceberg: the ones you see are not the only ones there. Behind each of your tier one suppliers (ie those suppliers with whom you have a direct contractual relationship) are all their suppliers (your tier two) and their suppliers' suppliers (your tier three). Suppliers are also like ice-crystals in that they are interconnected in intricate and not immediately visible structures – one company can be on each tier simultaneously as the goods and services it supplies are mixed and matched to meet your needs.

Then there are your other stakeholders: your customers, shareholders, regulators, legislators and pressure groups, both at home and abroad. Perhaps surprisingly many of these stakeholders will have something to say about why, what, how, when and where you buy. So if you don't set some direction and make it very vocal and crystal clear, these competing voices will fill the void.

Cascading sponsorship

Once you have determined how procurement can best support the achievement of your strategic ambition you need to keep at it. You need to particularly work the treacle layer (ie the stratum that exists in many organization where there is both empowerment and an incomplete view of the whole). Unless you win over or at least neutralize the treacle layer, procurement isn't going to play out exactly as you might have wished. When I was working as a consultant, I remember being very pleased when one of the senior stakeholders who sat in the treacle layer, said 'Yes' to something I was proposing. Pleased that is, until one of the client team told me that 'Yes' in his organization really meant that the stakeholder wasn't yet ready to say 'No'. Another tactic, which I am sure will be familiar to all of us, is for the stakeholder to say absolutely nothing – even to the most black and white of questions.

Therefore, I encourage you to cascade your sponsorship overtly and unequivocally. What this requires is that you 'walk the talk'. The treacle team is always looking out for the slightest sign that the boss doesn't really mean it! So if you say that cost-cutting is important then please cut cost; or if you say that we must act in a united fashion in respect of a supplier, make it so.

Similarly, if you can, measure the success of the initiative – whether that is cost-reduction, supplier management, innovation or something else. If it is measured, it can be managed. If it is managed, everyone in the organization will take it more seriously. If it is measured on the scorecard of the people who can make a difference to its success or failure, it is much more likely to be a success.

In summary

While this has been a short chapter, it is one of the key chapters to delivering success with procurement. It is both short and key because actually there isn't much to say about executive sponsorship beyond how critical it is, and always will be, to the success of procurement. You need to decide how procurement can best contribute to the strategic ambitions of your company, find the right way to communicate this to stakeholders within and outside the organization, and ensure that achievement of your procurement agenda is a measure that matters.

8 Strategy in context

Don't bother me with strategy, I don't have time

A couple of years ago I was talking to the corporate strategy team of a FTSE20 company in the UK and they were explaining their role to me. They said that in addition to developing group strategy, one of their key roles was going into individual business units (many of them equivalent in turnover to a FTSE100 company in their own right, by the way) and creating business strategies for the MD and their executive committee because, and here is the rub, they didn't have the time to do it for themselves.

Many of us don't have the luxury of a corporate strategy team but we do have access to consultants and it is often these consultants that lead our strategy formulation. Both corporate strategy teams and management consultants have a role to play in providing input to the top team as they determine their strategies. This input can be drawn from the analysis of the market, the competition and your existing capabilities, and will help the top team to determine their strategic response to the current and forecast environment. But let's face it, in a fast-paced business world where the market is primarily interested in our next quarter's performance, operational problem solving is a core competence and top priority of the modern business leader. The ability to fire-fight is often more highly prized in an organization than the creation of flame-retardant strategies.

In this chapter I will make the case for strategy. After all, if you don't have the time, patience or expertise to clearly articulate what 'good' looks like to your organization over the next five years, don't expect your organization and especially not its suppliers to either know or care. Therefore, we are going to explore the importance of articulating strategies for your organization, your supply chains and your suppliers; and particularly we will consider how these strategies can bind your suppliers to your success.

The value of strategy: the symphony orchestra

Imagine a company is like a symphony orchestra: various groups of well-trained specialists spread across a stage; musicians, some of whom are old-timers to the orchestra and others that are contract or guest artists; sheet music that shows bits of the whole; a paying and fickle audience; and the opportunity to cement or weaken the orchestra's reputation every time it performs. The challenge for the orchestra is how to make beautiful music and not just noise, and how to get everyone to play their part at the right time and to the best of their ability. What it needs is a strategy and this comes in the form of the score, the conductor, the principals and the oboe.

The score provides the blue print for the music that will be played by the entire orchestra. The full score is used by the conductor, while each musician will have sheet music for his or her part in the whole. The conductor is responsible for the interpretation of the music through rehearsals and performances as well as for cueing performers. He or she is visible to the whole orchestra and will provide cohesion and rhythm. Each section has a principal or leader to whom the rest of the section will look for leadership and upon whom the conductor will focus his or her instructions. The principal oboe is the one to whom the whole orchestra will tune their instruments.

Now imagine that the score is the strategy as agreed by the board; the conductor is the CEO bringing that strategy to life with his or her nuanced interpretation and communicating it through the layers of the organization, wielding a baton and cueing the activities of the various teams; and perhaps the oboe is the culture or values and, as such, provides the heartbeat and cohesion for the whole enterprise.

The case for strategy

As with the score for an orchestra, a clearly articulated strategy can be a unifying theme: a way for a high-performing organization to capture the hearts and minds of its employees, its customers and its suppliers. Without clear strategies, people who are further down the organization and trying to make sense of the whole will fill the void with partial solutions. Without clear strategy the whole is going to be less than the sum of its parts.

The process of formulating the strategy will also enable key personnel in the organization to test its appropriateness and veracity through a variety of lenses. In this way the strategies of the organization will be well thought through and their implications tested for their appropriateness to all areas of the company, its ambitions and the market within which it operates.

Strategies are a way of setting out for the whole world to see what is going to differentiate your company from the rest and what is important to you as an organization. They are the 'what' and not the 'how', the path and not the destination. Some contend that strategies are secret, something to be considered commercially sensitive and therefore given a blanket top secret stamp, but in reality there needs to be room for some flexibility here, depending upon their detail and specificity. A strategy could be to 'build deep customer-centred relationships', to 'concentrate on core activities', or to 'enter new markets in the emerging economics'. These strategies are ones that provide direction, approach and priorities and to my mind can and should be shared. The strategies that are commercially sensitive and need to played close to the chest are those that provide the 'how': buy this company or form a strategic alliance with that company, and I would suggest that there are not many people in an organization that need to be privy to these types of strategies before they are executed. Similarly, strategies on new product developments can be particularly sensitive and will be shared on a need-to-know basis. Interestingly, the need-to-know community will involve not only people within the organization but also key suppliers and manufacturers. The security around such initiatives will be achieved through various legal constructs such confidentiality and non-disclosure agreements.

So, direction-setting strategies should be shared openly with your employees, shareholders and suppliers. What you are letting them know is what 'good' looks like to your organization, which will help such stakeholder groups to figure out what their contribution could and should be to the attainment of the strategies. There is a great deal said about employees and suppliers not being proactive enough in their support of the organization they work with. Sometimes this is unfair criticism, especially if they are engaged with a company that is secretive about its business ambitions. Instead, sharing clear directional strategies that reveal what your priorities are and what you value will help stakeholders to figure out how best to make a contribution that could be meaningful to you. For example, your suppliers are more likely to bring their latest innovation to you if they know that your strategy is to differentiate your services by providing leading-edge solutions to your customers. Alternatively, they might propose ideas about process improvement and efficiency if they know that you want to achieve cost leadership above all things.

Cascading strategies

Delivery of the strategy is going to involve people and teams within the organization and outside. Cascading the strategy is the primary tool the top team have at their disposal for directing the activities of these units so that they operate in synchronization. By cascading strategies down through the organization, the top team can unify the company and its suppliers. For example, if the company wants to enter emerging markets this will be important information for various teams across the organization. The sales force may want to commission research into the customer response to their product in these new markets and, if there are vacancies, it might be best to recruit people who have experience of them. Similarly, the procurement department might be able to put business into these countries to help create a bridgehead to the new markets. The cascading process is one whereby the individual units take on board the overarching strategy and develop their own strategies to determine how their unit will contribute to the overall. A sound translation from the top team's overarching strategy to the specific strategies of functions and business units will increase the chances of achieving cohesive change across the organization.

Where strategies are not clearly articulated and communicated, functions and business units could inadvertently undermine each other and the overall company by developing incompatible and competing strategies. However, company-wide strategies that are clearly articulated and understood enable functions and business units to align their strategies in such a way that the overall ambitions of the organization are more likely to be achieved.

Cascading strategies into the extended enterprise

We have already established that you probably spend 50 per cent of your cost base with your suppliers and are therefore in effect spending as much with your suppliers as you do with your staff. While it is true that you are buying goods and services from these suppliers, what you are really doing is buying their expertise. Therefore when you are evaluating your ability to achieve your strategic ambition you must include your suppliers in your assessment. Consider this as your extended enterprise, and if you don't include your suppliers when doing this you are potentially underestimating the assets at your disposal by 50 per cent.

It makes it even crazier if you have decided that you are not going to share your strategies with your suppliers – effectively you have just tied one hand behind your back. If your suppliers understand what it is that you are aiming to achieve it stands to reasons that they are better placed to help you to achieve it. Knowing your strategy should give them the incentive to look for greater opportunities, and ones that you may not have considered yourself, for them to add value to your organization.

Collaborating strategically with key suppliers will also help you to better understand one another. It is very easy, because you have a commercial relationship with suppliers, to assume that you know who they are. However, suppliers are often more complex organizations than you might think and just because you buy one service from them in one country doesn't mean that they don't have other services in other geographies that might be helpful to you. A simple example of this is the expansion of companies that started life as IT outsource providers, such as Infosys and Wipro, who are widely recognized for providing IT services and back office processing in India but who now have operations spread across other geographies and have started expanding into added-value services such as the world of management consultancy.

Cascading strategy into your supply chains

It is also important that you evaluate the supply chains you are responsible for in pursuit of the company's strategies. You need to assess whether or not your supply chains are capable of furthering the company's ambitions. For example, your strategies may require changes in technology (delivering product innovation or process improvement), volume (either growing or shrinking) and geographical focus (new or existing markets). Similarly, you will need to decide whether or not you need to construct additional supply chains in pursuit of new strategic objectives.

As was mentioned in an earlier chapter, research has revealed that the further away in the supply chain a supplier is from the customer the more static the supply chain seems to that supplier. This reinforces the importance for any organization of proactively communicating its strategic priorities to suppliers that are fundamental to its success and encouraging them to inform their own suppliers.

While I have talked a lot about cascading strategies in this chapter, it is worth noting that, especially while the strategies are being formulated, there will be a lot of information ascending from the supply chains, suppliers, functions and business units to ensure that the strategies being formulated in the upper reaches of the organization are appropriate.

In summary

An overarching strategy for your company provides the guidance that your stakeholders need to determine how they can contribute effectively to your success. It is important that the strategies are owned and disseminated by your executive. While some components of your strategies will be confidential, the rest should be cascaded widely to all stakeholders, including your suppliers. The time needed to develop and disseminate strategy to your extended enterprise may be difficult to find when faced with operational concerns, but time spent on strategy is likely to be the most valuable moments in your working day.

9 Knowing what the business needs

It's never too early to know what you need

To know and articulate what you need seems very simple, yet it can be the first hurdle that trips us up. Just ask yourself how often you have called for help before you either know what the problem is or what you would most value from any solution. Similarly, how many projects fail because you didn't really know what you set out to do in the first place or what 'good' would look like once it was done?

This goes back to some of the themes we explored earlier in this book: our job as leaders is to lead, and beyond the odd call of, 'Follow me people, I am right behind you!' this usually requires us to know where we are going. However, as leaders we are often very action-oriented and this unfortunately can mean that we act before we think. If we do so, then at best our teams, including our suppliers, will think for us and potentially deliver something that is ok but not really what we needed. At worst, no one thinks, we all act, and as a result no one gets anything of value apart from you – a big bill and not much to show for it.

My husband Howard was in a meeting some years ago pitching to deliver an IT solution to a blue chip company. His colleague took two things into the meeting: a 200-page response to the brief he had been given and a black velvet pouch that clearly had something in it. Over the course of the meeting Howard's colleague managed to persuade the client that he wanted the unknown contents of the pouch rather than the known contents of the response document. And who wouldn't? Most of us like to think that there is something much better out there, something that we haven't thought of yet, the silver bullet. Of course we don't want to be closed to new ideas and miss opportunities, but we have to recognize that suppliers have a product to sell and will do that by promoting the wonderful features that differentiate it from its competitors' offerings. Unless we have a crystal clear view of our need, we can end up paying for things that may be nice to have but add little or no value. Too often in business, a supplier will find and fixate on the solution, and if you as a buyer don't really know what you need then you can end up acquiring that solution because it is there and not because it is the right solution for your company.

In this chapter we are going to explore the value of clearly establishing your business need before you start to think about how to meet it, and how to figure out when you need to standardize and when you need to innovate.

Articulating the need

Taking the time to know what you need will pay dividends. For the hours, days or months that you spend as an organization figuring this out, you will benefit a hundred-fold. I am not proposing analysis paralysis or protracted stakeholder engagement, indeed if you can sit down and clearly articulate the business need, then do it now. The challenge is that often this need isn't properly understood or articulated. A poorly specified need can create an opportunity for your suppliers to mould it to fit their capability, and your lack of clarity will deny you the rigour to spot and stop this.

I use the word 'need' very carefully: I am not talking about what you want or wish for (this is where the hobbyists come out to play). Ask an engineer what he or she wants and you will probably have a full technical specification in the blink of an eye; or a marketer and you will probably be given the glossy concepts of a new campaign launch. Business need is all about avoiding the wishes and the wants and instead is about distilling the essence of the requirement. A business doesn't need an air conditioning unit, it needs acclimatization; a business doesn't need a laptop, it needs personal productivity tools; a business doesn't need an advertising campaign, it needs increased sales and greater brand awareness.

At times it can be as important to express what it is that you don't want as it is to say what you do. A couple of years ago I listened to J K

Rowling talking about creating and making believable the world of Harry Potter. She said that what is as important as describing what can happen in a believable world of magic, is letting the reader know what can't happen. In other words, it is vital to establish the boundaries. If anything and everything can happen then people will struggle to believe the world because they cannot understand its parameters. If the author establishes both what can happen and what cannot, then the readers can start to understand, and when they can understand they can more easily believe.

The same happens in business when you are launching a new product offering. Despite the temptation, it can be disastrous if the product is oversold. I remember a few years ago discussing a new service offering that we were going to launch in management consulting. I thought it was a really intriguing service, but the more questions I asked and the more affirmations I received that 'Yes, yes, it could do that,' the more nervous and sceptical I became. I needed to know the boundaries and limitations to understand the offer and make its qualities believable.

Articulating need can be harder to do than you might think (which is probably why we often don't do it as thoroughly as we should). There are several reasons for this. First, it is unlikely that one person can articulate the need statement in splendid isolation. In reality there will be a variety of stakeholders that need to be engaged in the process, and as the conversation evolves our ideas will develop and change, which is of course a good thing and the real value of the discussion. That said, corralling and wordsmithing all the stakeholder views into a single cohesive needs statement can be painful. At times, trying to nail down a needs statement can be like trying to hit a moving target.

Second, people tend to think in solutions by imagining what the end result will look like. Once again, that shouldn't be a problem as long as the solution isn't then specified as the need. Rather, the specification should be used to test the appropriateness of the needs statement – not replace it. Finally, it is easy to get your need statement tangled up with research and development.

Who needs blue sky?

Research and development (R&D) is a much used and abused term. Contrary to popular belief, R&D happens all over the place and not just in the R&D departments. It can pop up all over your supply chains and your organization (which is a good thing if it is recognized and controlled).

As the phrase implies, research should come before development, but the two can get jumbled up with sometimes disastrous consequences, especially to budgets and timescales. This happens when you think you have nailed the need (possibly with input from the research stage) and you are now in development, and suddenly more research is commissioned. An obvious example of this is where, after the functional specifications (needs statements in our speak) has been signed off, the enhancements keep coming.

I think it is useful to see research and development as a three-step process rather than the two it claims to be. Research is the time for the blue sky thinking, the gestating of ideas and the scientific investigation. It can result in solutions looking for problems or hypotheses waiting for evidence. It can also start with a needs statement or be the research undertaken to discover and articulate a need.

The second step in the process is the stage gate. This is the hurdle that has to be jumped before serious time, money and effort are committed to develop it into a full-blown solution or product. The key to this stage is to have a clearly articulated needs statement. To progress through the stage gate and pass onto the third step in the process, development, you have to have a well-defined need and corresponding solution with a fully scoped out budget. The final stage, development, is then the step where the serious investment is made and from which you are looking to deliver a proposition that does what it's supposed to do, within the time frame and to the budget you have agreed.

In 1942, during World War II, chemists were working in Eastman Kodak trying to make an extra-clear plastic for precision gun-sights. I don't know if they ever succeeded in developing the plastic they were seeking, but one by-product of their research was the invention of cyanoacrylate adhesive – better known to you and me as 'super glue'. In effect they were trying to find a solution for one need and found something that didn't have one but was still very interesting. So, rather than being distracted, this invention was filed away somewhere for almost 10 years before Harry Coover, its inventor, started work on it again. Presumably, Mr Coover realized then that he had discovered a chemical that could meet a real-world need. It took until 1956 before a patent was filed and 1958 before it went into commercial production.

Google, with its reputation for creativity and innovation, also has an interesting approach to R&D. It famously has a system whereby its employees have a day a week free to work on whatever they want to. Google adopted this idea from the academic world, where professors at universities typically have a day a week free for their own research. Google has over the years attracted some of the brightest talents across the world and having one's own pet research project has become a must-have if an employee wants credibility and a good appraisal at the year end. This ticks the research box. What Google has also introduced is a hopper for these research projects that introduces increasingly rigorous hurdles to be overcome before the idea can gestate into a development project. Google has a very active research mentality but it also has a rigorous mechanism to ensure delivery of high quality products that satisfy the company's needs (Vise, 2005).

Bringing suppliers into the mix

So, R&D occurs across your organization and structuring it with stage gates helps to improve the quality of the deliverables. Understanding where you are in the process will also promote fruitful interaction with your suppliers. When you ask a supplier to deliver innovation to you, make sure that it clearly understands your requirements and the problems you are trying to solve. In this way the supplier will focus its energy on things that are important to you and hopefully come up with something that will work for you and for it.

Sharing information on strategies, priorities and process will encourage suppliers to participate in your projects. Sharing information can be very difficult to do appropriately and well. When we are immersed in our own organization, its vision, strategy and priorities, we can assume that our suppliers already know this stuff, or we are nervous of sharing information outside the company, which makes us appear secretive and remote. All this means that we just don't share as much timely information as we could. However, there is evidence to indicate that if we did share information more appropriately, suppliers could add much more value to our business and its relationships.

A few years ago, Proctor & Gamble (P&G) was known as one of the more private organizations and, like many large, long-standing companies, distrusted things that 'were not invented here'. In 2000 less than 15 per cent of its innovations involved outside parties, but by 2008 this had grown to 50 per cent. The credit for this transformation rests with A G Lafley, who adopted a variety of strategies on becoming CEO in 2000. These included putting the consumer at the heart of everything and embracing the concept of 'open innovation', whereby P&G sought to attract innovation from outside the company. In an interview with the Harvard Business School, Mr Lafley recognized that, 'While P&G is very good at developing, qualifying, and commercializing innovation, we're not necessarily any better than others at creating it' (Alumni Achievement Awards, 2009).

Open innovation requires companies that embrace the philosophy to make themselves easy to do business with and more communicative in respect of ambitions and strategies than they might have been in the past. P&G has developed Open + Develop, which is its programme of open innovation. This is a process for sharing both inbound and outbound innovation. On the inbound side, P&G publishes its needs on the Open + Develop website (www.pgconnectdevelop.com) for potential partners to browse and submit their solutions. It is worth looking at the website to see examples of well-defined needs statements. On the outbound side, P&G publishes a list of the assets it has available for partners to license. P&G has come a long way since 2000, and by 2009 it had over a 1,000 agreements with its partners, which range from individuals to Fortune 500 companies.

One of the most challenging aspects of shared innovation in my experience is making sure that priorities and challenges are communicated effectively. Nine times out of 10 when I ask a colleague what he or she thinks about a supplier and its contribution to his or her business, that colleague will bemoan the fact that the supplier isn't particularly innovative or proactive in identifying improvement opportunities. I think this is because this notion of innovation is too vague for any supplier to do much about.

I have been guilty of expressing similar sentiments to suppliers, even holding workshops with them and achieving very little. Having analysed this, I went wrong because I was never very specific about what the innovation should deliver (eg breakthrough technology, lower cost, greater productivity) or how I would go about implementing it. With this woolly remit, the suppliers would work very hard to come up with new ideas – often impacting things that I didn't care about, and instead of being proactive and providing this feedback, I was silent. The suppliers got huffy and it all reinforced my perception that the suppliers just weren't very good at innovation. This was a nightmare of my own making.

So, having learnt my lesson, I now ensure that the supplier knows what is important to the organization and therefore where to concentrate its creative energy. Ok, the areas might be routine ones – time to market, unit cost, increased reliability, and better processing capability – but if the supplier does come up with good ideas, they are ones that I can progress because they are tackling the genuine and recognized challenges that face my business.

The complexities of needs statements

In the 1940s, Abraham Maslow wrote a theory on human motivation, popularly known as his 'hierarchy of need' (Maslow, 1943). In it Maslow identified five levels of need, from the most basic required to support life to those that give it meaning and purpose. Briefly these are physiological (breathing, food and shelter); safety (security and health); social (friendship and family); esteem (of self and by others) and self-actualization (becoming all that one can be).

Maslow's hierarchy of need is used in marketing training to offer insights into a consumer's motives for action. The idea is that the more a developer and marketer can position a product to meet a recognized need, the more consumers will see the product as valuable to them.

A similar hierarchy of needs can be constructed for a company and its supply chains. At the most basic level the company must be capable of survival – and this is all about revenue, profitability and cash flow. Then comes the need for market positioning and market share, followed by brand recognition and product value, and ultimately the ambition to be the best the company can be. Therefore to be successful a supply chain must recognize and align with the company's hierarchy of needs.

A needs statement will have a variety of components. It should contain information on what both your customers and you value about the good or service, reflect any regulatory and environmental requirements and have something about target profit and cost. The needs statement should be regularly revisited, especially to reflect changes in the market. It should not have anything in it that indicates 'how' something should be done ; it should concentrate on the 'what' and 'why'.

Needs statements are the starting point. Once you know the need, you can start figuring out (ideally with your suppliers and other stakeholders) how to satisfy it. And now you can be as true blue sky in your thinking as you want because the litmus test is defined: does it satisfy the need?

Primary and secondary supply chains

If you cast your mind back to earlier concepts in this book, you should have an idea of where I am going with this. There is a hierarchy of needs statements associated with tiers of supply chains and it is very important to establish them appropriately before you start to figure out how best to deliver them. It is important because the value and cost of the primary supply chain is naturally going to be much greater than any of the secondary or tertiary supply chains that support it. Therefore it is the primary supply chain that all others should be designed to safeguard and enhance in the first instance, and only then optimized in their own right. One way of ensuring this is to establish the need of each layer in the context of those above it.

A simple example for a bank would be its cash dispensers. If you buy cash dispensers that hold so much money that the supplier who delivers the cash is unwilling to fill it because of security concerns, or that hold too little money so they run out every weekend and the bank's customers have to go elsewhere, then you can imagine that the consequences on the primary supply chain are going to be significant and unpleasant.

I came across an interesting example of this type of 'unintended consequence' when I was running a project that I mentioned earlier in this book. It was the project looking at how supply chain management could extend the life expectancy of the North Sea oil and gas industry. As part of this project I met with a wireline operator. This is a supplier that lowers tools down oil and gas wells in order to evaluate the reservoirs. The latest, leading-edge (even bleeding-edge) technology and tools are used to provide information to enable the oil companies to get the most out of their oil and gas wells. I was there to help them analyse their supply chain with a view to optimizing it and to understand how it interfaced with the primary supply chain it served, which was 'Drill a well'.

Oil companies that are involved in exploration and production are, in my experience, unusual in the world of business because they believe that their competitive advantage is in their core business, finding and extracting oil, and that the best thing they can do about all the other activities they have to undertake is to make them as cost-efficient as possible. This means that they are willing to spend zillions on anything that promises to improve their ability to hone their competitive advantage and want to spend as little as possible on every-thing else. Because of this they are by instinct very collaborative organizations. One consequence of this for the North Sea was that several of the oil companies got together to pool their logistics operations – particularly aircraft and supply vessels. They agreed 'milk runs' whereby the helicopters and ships visited the oil platforms sequentially, regardless of their owners. This significantly reduced the cost of operation for each participant – so far so good.

However, as I found out when I helped the wireline operator to analyse its supply chain, these milk runs had unanticipated consequences for both them and the whole 'Drill a well' primary supply chain. One of the implications of the shared logistics was that the schedule of visits to the various platforms was less frequent than historically and therefore both people and equipment had to stay offshore longer. This meant that staff and equipment from the wireline operator had to stay offshore for several days after they had completed the job. The unintended consequence of this was that the supplier was forced to increase inventory to meet its customers' needs. The extra cost of inventory meant that the supplier had less money available to invest in the latest technology, even though the latest technology was what the oil companies really valued in their mission to find and extract maximum oil and gas. The oil companies didn't know this because they had never really analysed the consequences, and the supplier didn't tell them because it might have meant that it lost the contract or had to share work with rivals.

The Kindle

The Kindle is Amazon's proprietary reader for eBooks and other digital media. It was first introduced in the United States in November 2007 and launched internationally in October 2009. The take-up of eBooks has been rapid, with Amazon reporting that, where e-versions are available, they already equate to a third of the market. Just after its publication, sales of the eBook version of Dan Brown's novel *The Lost Symbol* were outstripping demand for the paper version.

In October 2009, Jeff Bezos, the founder of Amazon.com and its chief executive, said: 'Our vision for Kindle is every book ever printed, in print or out of print, in every language, all available within 60 seconds' (Gallo, 2009). This is a pretty good needs statement for a primary supply chain (see Figure 9.1) as it establishes some important parameters. For example, we know that Amazon needs access to electronic versions of every book, regardless of origin, age or language, which can then be downloaded to the Kindle within a minute. This, combined with some cost and development targets, will give all stakeholders, whether customers, employees or potential suppliers, a pretty good idea of what is important to Amazon.

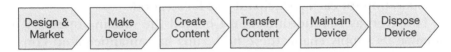

Figure 9.1   Primary supply chain of the Amazon Kindle

Interestingly, the desire to have all the world's books available to the Kindle user could have significant implications for the product. For example, the Kindle uses proprietary software and design formats and is not as open as other generic readers. The Kindle, unlike other readers such as the Sony eReader, is tied to Amazon and cannot receive content that is not produced to its proprietary standards. This could be a burden in the longer term to the Kindle; if Amazon is to achieve its vision, it will have to have created unique versions of every book. If it had adopted an open technology, it could use and sell e-content created to open standards and tap into the broader market.

Amazon realizes that customers of the Kindle will value its content rather than the device, and is using this to lock-in sales for Amazon. Therefore a design principle of the Kindle is that all content must be sourced from Amazon because of its proprietary technology. This, though, has a variety of consequences for the supply chain: it puts a huge burden on Amazon to become a one-stop shop to meet all its customers' needs and it is building in costs that its rivals do not necessarily have to incur. However, it does mean that, at the moment, a customer who buys a Kindle is tied to Amazon to provide all the content.

You might be wondering whether Amazon's strategy is right or not, and to answer that question I would like to introduce here the element of time. Years ago, products and their associated supply chains lasted a lot longer than they do now. Products would be launched on the market (hopefully enjoying premium prices that reflected the originality and desirability of the gizmo) and over time the supply chain would be refined to reduce its cost – often with the ambition of safeguarding margins as consumer ennui and market competition eroded the achievable unit price. Nowadays there are some products and supply chains that have a shelf-life of months rather than years – for example, cell/mobile phones are only used for an average of 18 months before being replaced.

Against this backdrop I would contest that Amazon's strategy is very savvy. Amazon is at the forefront of a new market where both the equipment and the content need to be designed and built from scratch and where neither the equipment nor the content is useful in isolation from the other. Manufacturers of e-Readers play only a part in the generic supply chain. Amazon owns its supply chain. Sony and other manufacturers need open standards to stimulate the sales of their machines as they need to encourage other suppliers to create content and stimulate the growth of their market. Amazon has proprietary standards because it is already known for content, and by owning the machines and the content it has provided itself with the opportunity to both create and exploit the full supply chain.

This opens up an intriguing possibility in the way that Amazon might position Kindle in the future. It could deploy a similar business strategy to the one used by the manufacturers of the printers that we use at home. The printers themselves are increasingly cheap to buy because the supply chain owner makes its money on the proprietary printer cartridges that we must then purchase. The total cost of ownership to the customer is driven more by the cost of the replacement cartridges than it is by the acquisition cost of the printer. Indeed you could go so far as to say that the print device itself is the loss-leader in the supply chain.

Over time one could imagine an evolution of Amazon's strategy either in line with the printer market, whereby the Kindle becomes the loss leader and the eBooks the equivalent of the ink cartridge, or where the Kindle and its owners adopt open standards to exploit not only its e-Reader market share but also that of their rivals. It's going to be interesting to watch what happens.

In summary

The more clearly you can articulate what you need to your suppliers, the greater the chance they have of fulfilling it. The statement of your needs should focus on describing the 'what' and the 'why', thereby giving your supplier the latitude to innovate within clear boundaries as it consider the best ways it can satisfy your needs.

Research and development are activities that go on throughout organizations. Separating them with a stage gate process will improve the quality of new products and services. Explaining where you are in the research and development process helps when you are involving suppliers, as does openly sharing information on your intentions, problems and opportunities. Open innovation is key here.

A complex supply chain is structured in a hierarchy of primary, secondary and so forth supply chains. Each level in the hierarchy is designed to satisfy a need and therefore the needs are themselves structured in a hierarchy. To avoid any unintended consequences of changes, the needs of each layer in the hierarchy must be established in the context of the needs of those above it.

10 Picking the right suppliers

Now I want to move on to explore how to pick the best suppliers and put in place the most appropriate contracts to deliver your value proposition. It goes without saying that you are always going to select and reward suppliers that can help to deliver your offer and enhance your brand. You are going to tell them what you need from them, when you need it and how much you will pay for it. They will figure out how best to fulfil this need and make a profit.

The challenge is that you are likely to need different suppliers and contractual terms at various points in the maturity of the market within which you are operating. For example, at some point, in order to avoid being commoditized by your customers you will seek to differentiate your brand and your solution – in which case you will be looking for suppliers that can help you to achieve this. On the other hand, and possibly once your offer has already been commoditized, you might seek to become cost leaders, in which case you will need suppliers that can deliver cost advantage.

So, the way you construct your supply chain will be determined by where the good or service you offer is on its market maturity curve. In this chapter I am going to introduce a model for mapping your product or service onto the market maturity curve and then go on to look at a couple of examples that will show the theory in practice.

Your supply chain on the maturity curve

As an offer travels through its life from inception to retirement, it moves along a maturity curve. Figure 10.1 illustrates this progress; the maturity journey is indicated by the arrow. Where your product or service sits on this journey will have a big influence on your supply chain, the type of suppliers you want to work with and the contracts you put in place.

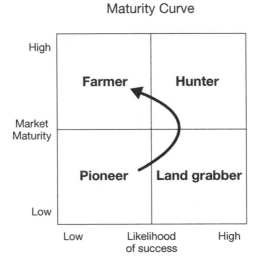

Figure 10.1 The market maturity curve

The two dimensions of the diagram are 'market maturity' and 'likelihood of success'. By *maturity* I mean the position of the good or service in respect of its customer base – if emerging or embryonic in the eyes of the customer, it will be low on the axis. If it has become a 'must have' it would be very high. By *likelihood of success* I include elements like product take-up, degree of competition and your position in the market (however mature or immature that is).

One of the first things we need to figure out is the market in which our offer will sit and this is tricky because markets morph, segment and coalesce. A hundred years ago there was probably a single automotive market and all the automobiles would have been sitting in 'pioneer' in Figure 10.1. Today, that market is segmented into a dozen or so markets such as Sports Utility Vehicles (likely to be a 'farmer' in the diagram), electric cars (pioneer) and compacts (hunter); the quadrants are discussed below. As this indicates, you are probably going to have a better understanding of what market you are in when it is more mature. In its early stages the market is almost certain to be more dynamic and ill-defined – both of which are in themselves characteristics of the pioneer market.

Pioneer

This reflects an exciting and possibly scary combination of immature market and risky business venture. When you are selecting suppliers to work in your supply chain they are likely to be very strategically aligned to your ambitions and leaders in the areas in which you need their expertise (by the way, don't be distracted by those suppliers that are good at things that you don't really need). Your suppliers are not necessarily scale players and indeed they might be niche providers or start-ups. Your contracts are likely to be short in duration, with reward structures aligned to joint success, and will pay only for what you use.

Land grabber

The market is still relatively immature but you think you are onto something. You need to get your supply chain well positioned for a growing market. You will be looking for suppliers that can help you dominate the market as it matures by providing things like scale and established distribution channels or routes to the customer. Suppliers you used in the pioneer phase could be growing with you, but others might need to be shored up by other sources of supply or even weeded out. Your contracts are likely to be longer term and reward structures will still be aligned to joint success (when wouldn't they?), though joint success may now look different. While you will probably be still paying for use, you might also start thinking about paying for capacity.

Hunter

The market has matured and you are still really well positioned to make the most of it. However, you might be starting to think about market segmentation, new geographies and product differentiation – all to enable you to pick off any high-margin business and premium custom. Your ideal suppliers will be those that can help you to keep your product offering fresh and appealing and break into new areas of the market, thereby keeping your market share relatively high and always profitable. You are honing your supply chain in this phase, getting it fit for a much more mature market with savvy customers, smarter competition and more challenging prices. You still have options on differentiation and cost leadership and you need suppliers that can support the options you select. However, your contracts will now vary, depending on your suppliers, which might be agile and innovative so as to deliver product breakthroughs or productivity-oriented cost leadership.

Farmer

The market has matured and is probably saturated. Your customers are more demanding and your opportunities for making money are becoming harder. Your focus in this market is less about innovation and more about evolution. You will be evolving your products to keep them attractive but simultaneously managing your production processes to ensure you are cost-competitive. Any breakthrough technology will most likely result in a new supply chain in a new market – kicking off the whole cycle again. Your suppliers are likely to be cost-advantaged to ensure your supply chain can remain cost-competitive as the product becomes commoditized. If you haven't already, you might consider low-cost sourcing overseas. You might consider contracting out the whole production to another company, as happens often in high-tech and pharmaceuticals organizations. The focus is on cost as well as continuous and incremental improvement.

Obviously, there are huge underlying complexities – both the benefit and the curse of two-by-twos is that they make things simple and sometimes too simple. For example, a market can move so rapidly that to be successful you need to think about the whole lifecycle from the very beginning of your journey; or a new entrant that has both attractive products and lowest costs can blow up your game plan at any moment. That said, let's look at some examples of how this model has worked in practice.

In practice

Acorn

My first example started life as Cambridge Processor Unit Ltd (CPU), which was set up in England in the late 1970s. It went from a profit of

£3,000 in its first year to £8.6 million in the summer of 1983 on the back of the success of the BBC Micro, a computer tied into a seminal British Broadcasting Company (BBC) programme on how to programme computers. It floated later in that year and changed its name to Acorn Computer Group plc with Acorn Computers Ltd as its microcomputer division. Also in 1983 it launched its new PC, the Acorn Electron, and after a very successful Christmas marketing campaign had an order book for 300,000 units. Unfortunately, production line problems meant that its suppliers only managed to deliver 30,000 units, thereby failing to sate the Christmas demand, which was soaked up elsewhere when parents bought their children other home computers such as the Commodore 64 and the ZX Spectrum (both now icons of a past computer age).

The problems were further compounded in 1984 when the home computer market collapsed (possibly due to market saturation, as there wasn't an awful lot that the typical home user could do with a computer in 1984 – how the world has changed!) Ironically, this happened just as Acorn's production problems were solved and its 300,000 Electrons were successfully made and delivered to Acorn. Unfortunately the contracts that the company had established with its suppliers meant that it couldn't turn off the supply and it very soon had a huge and costly unsold inventory that it had to house and care for. All of this contributed to a perfect storm at Acorn and within a very short space of time the company had sold a majority stake to Olivetti.

What is interesting though is that the failure of Acorn's supply chain in late 1983 and, ironically, the same supply chain's 'success' in 1984, together with poor quality contracts that hadn't anticipated any downturn in sales, caused the company to flounder (Shillingford, 2001).

Great things continued to come out of the Acorn stable, many of them very much ahead of their time. These included set-top boxes that anticipated the on-demand video market by possibly 20 years and collaborations in the world of network PCs that must be, at least partially, the forefather of the latest buzz of cloud computing. Probably most successful of them all has been ARM, which started life in 1990 as a joint venture of Acorn Computers, Apple Computer and VLSI Technologies (a long-term supplier to Acorn). This company designs low-power microprocessors and licenses the intellectual property to chip manufacturers. As such it has been market dominant in the field of mobile phone chips for many years.

Tom Hohenberg, Acorn's former marketing manager and the man responsible for the campaign that built the demand at Christmas1983, explained why the Electron foundered: 'Missing the boat that Christmas deprived it of the critical mass needed to get the best software developed for it.' This statement reflects one of the basic messages in this book – the need to understand what your customers value about your product. As I have said already, there were very limited uses for computers in the early 1980s. What happened to the Acorn Electron demonstrates that the failure to create critical mass ('land grab') meant that software companies were unwilling to invest in creating the value-added applications (such as computer games) it needed for its customers, and as such the market for the enabling device – the Electron – withered (Sturgeon, 2002).

Interestingly, though possibly coincidentally, ARM Ltd has thrived partly because of its strategy to downward compatibility, and open systems mean that the company is no longer tied to software applications specific to its technology. In an open standards environment it is able to compete directly based on the attributes of its microprocessors (Eda and Shintoh, 2002).

Intel

Intel was formed in the late 1960s and while it was credited with the invention of the first commercial microprocessing chip in 1971, it initially made its name as a manufacturer of memory. By the early 1980s increased competition, primarily from Japan, had commoditized the market for memory chips and this was impacting profits – it was becoming a 'farmer's' market. This, together with the growth of the PC market, encouraged Andy Grove, Intel's then CEO, to change the focus of his company to the development of microprocessors, which was then entering 'land grab'.

In 1983, when Intel's shift of focus occurred, manufacturing of complex integrated circuits was rather unreliable and therefore every buyer made sure that it had several suppliers under contract to safeguard supply of this critical component. Intel decided that it would challenge this procurement approach head-on through a dual strategy of improving the quality of manufacture (it established three large factories in different parts of the United States) and stopping the license of its designs to other manufacturers. In effect, Grove's strategy was to first 'land grab', then 'hunt' and, through a variety of strategies, to stay in these highly profitable states as long as possible. These other strategies included technological advance – after all, Moore's Law, that computing power will double every two years, came from the founder of Intel (see http://download.intel.com/museum/Moores_Law/ Printed_Materials/Moores_Law_Backgrounder.pdf).

The most recent innovations from Intel have been the Intel Atom™ processor used in a variety of products including netbooks, and its own netbook, the classmate PC. Interestingly, while Intel remains true to Grove's desire to keep microprocessor manufacturing in-house (it now has 15 wafer fabrication plants worldwide), its approach to the classmate PC is dramatically different. While every classmate PC marked 'Intel Inside', there is a network of country-specific manufacturers and other technology partners (referred to as the 'Alliance') to develop and satisfy local demands. For example, in the UK, the local manufacturer produces them as Fizzbooks; in India as the Connoi Convertible Classmate PC; in China there are two manufacturers; and in the United States four. In all cases, with the exception of the 'Intel Inside', the brand names are different and peripheral specifications vary.

This is an interesting strategy for 'land grab'. With a billion school children globally as the target market for netbooks, Intel is utilizing local manufacturers, technology companies and distribution channels to help make its product attractive to the local market, appropriately supported and with country-specific applications. I suppose this brings home the point that just because the market is an emerging one it isn't necessarily small!

In summary

While puppies may be for life and not just for Christmas, this is not true for either suppliers or contracts. As the supply chain owner goes through the market maturity curve, he or she must tailor both the sources of supply and the contract terms to ensure his or her offering continues to exploit the opportunities the market presents. While some suppliers will go on the whole journey, others will come and go, and success will be determined by making the right choices along the way.

11 Understanding your spend

One size doesn't fit all

You have just found out that you spend millions (if not billions) with your suppliers. You have zillions of suppliers and thousands of employees. Your P&L could really do with an injection of cost reduction to the bottom line and some real innovation to the top. You have just bought into the concept that procurement may be able to help and I have just laid the responsibility for direction setting and sponsorship firmly at your door – but where on earth should you start?

Don't panic, help is at hand. The Pareto principle could have been designed for procurement: its 80/20 rule was rarely more applicable. Even if you haven't paid much attention to procurement in your organization, you are very likely to have 80 per cent of your spend with no more than 20 per cent of your suppliers and 20 per cent of that 20 per cent will be important to you.

However, before you start breathing normally again and put the brown paper bag away, I should also point out that there are lots of other more important lenses to look through when determining where you should start; for example your key supply chains and critical suppliers. You may not spend much money on these and (this is where the hyperventilation might start again) you may not be that important to the suppliers of these business-critical services and solutions. You may even have a monopoly supplier who actually doesn't care about your organization or its success.

In this chapter we will explore how you can analyse your external spend for opportunity and risk, spot the critical suppliers and assess their attitude to you as a customer.

Alien tactics

Imagine that you are an alien approaching Earth for the first time. I guess that you would begin with having a good look at the whole planet from space – to get the lie of the land (so to speak). Then you might start to classify things – land, water, atmosphere; and then to categorize them further – land into mountains, plains, desert and icepacks; water into seas, lakes and rivers; atmosphere into oxygen, nitrogen, etc. At some point you would probably look at how these things interact, what their uses are and who or what uses them. Ultimately you would figure out what, if anything, was useful to you. I think this is a pretty good analogy for an organization that is looking at its third-party spend for the first time: you categorize, classify and quantify your spend, you figure out how it is used now and ultimately assess its future usefulness. Assuming the alien has good intentions, it will probably start to think about how to get what it wants by figuring out what it has to trade... but I think this is probably stretching the parallel too far. So let's abandon the space ship for a moment and head to the accounts payable team instead.

The first thing you probably want to know is how much you spend in total. As payments vary through the year – with ad hoc purchases, monthly and quarterly rentals, etc – you should pick a period that makes sense as your baseline. I would suggest 12 months. If you haven't really studied your spend before, concentrate on the things you know: the suppliers you pay, the departments that spend the money and the general ledger codes your company uses to break down costs for budgeting and tracking purposes.

This is the first ah-ha moment – do you remember the banker who told me that the bank didn't spend money because it didn't make anything, and the reaction to the news that it actually spent £2 billion despite not making anything? Trust me, these few snippets of information will get a good conversation going in any boardroom. Imagine the conversation: 'We spend 50 per cent of our direct costs with over 500 different suppliers but use more than 6,000 suppliers overall; most of our money is spent by your department, Fred; we are spending 20 per cent alone on travel – particularly the corporate jet is costing us…'. I jest somewhat – although the only time I got the full attention of one boardroom was when I was responsible for developing a new travel strategy and there was a corporate jet at stake!

In reality what you have with these few pieces of information is the alien's first step to understanding Earth, its masses and its quantities. This is the time when you can figure out for yourself whether or not third-party spend is worth pursuing as an opportunity to reduce costs. The less this information has been looked at holistically, the greater the opportunity. Beware the enthusiast who talks about the good departmental deals that have been done – they will be there, but a deal done with little knowledge of the bigger company-wide picture will always have room for improvement.

It is also a good time to look at the suppliers with which you spend most money – some will come as a complete shock, especially if as part of your analysis you have linked together all the suppliers that are part of the same corporation and reported them as one. Don't be fooled though: expenditure alone doesn't always identify which suppliers are important to your business and your customers, and I will introduce some other techniques to help with this later in the chapter. Depending on the business you are in, you could look to see which of these suppliers are also your customers. I am not keen on reciprocity as it can drive both entities to making suboptimal decisions – but as a factor, it is important to know.

I am working on the assumption that you don't have a procurement system for recording requests, orders and receipts at the moment or that if you do, it will provide an incomplete picture of your expenditure. However if you do, this is obviously a better data source to interrogate for information on who spends what with which suppliers. In this case you will probably have a formal category structure to help classify your expenditure. On the assumption that your accounts payable system and general ledger provide the best overall data (frequently the case, in my experience), these should, despite the limitations of all general ledger classifications, provide a reasonable outline of your spend. The management information will have helped to identify the departments with the largest spend and this will allow you to focus on particular stakeholders who you might need to win over to your procurement improvement exercise.

Regardless of whether you have a purchasing system or have to rely on other sources, be wary of those areas of spend that are most scrutinized by the board, such as marketing and consultancy, as you could find that spend against these lines is slender and, mysteriously, the incidence of misclassification is high. I once found the acquisition of a hot air balloon for marketing recorded as an IT peripheral.

Value

A few months ago I was completing a crossword. It was not a cryptic one, which I confess are way beyond my ability, but a simple, complete-over-coffee crossword that gives you one word or phrase and you have to identify a word or phrase that has the same meaning. The clue was 'cost' and the answer was five letters long. Even after I got the letter 'p' as the first letter, I was absolutely stumped. Eventually though I had to accept that the answer was 'price'. I was somewhat outraged because to me the clue was completely misleading. Cost and price are not the same by any stretch of imagination. In fact I would go so far as to say that beyond their use in calculating the profitability of something there is really very little correlation between the two words at all. To all those crossword compilers out there I would say that the same applies to the words 'expenditure' and 'value'. These words are not synonymous and in procurement, woe betide anyone who thinks that they are.

Once you have classified your expenditure and you know how much you are spending on particular goods and services (this is probably the next level of analysis down from your general ledger codes), you need to understand not only the absolute spend but also its value to your organization. Figuring out what is important to your organization about what you buy or who you buy it from is not something you can or should do in splendid isolation – wherever you sit in the organization. This is because supply chains exist to meet the requirements of your customers or colleagues; they involve tiers of suppliers, some of whom are more visible to you than others; and they involve various stakeholders across your organization. Not only is it essential to get all the stakeholders involved, I have found that there is something really magical about getting them together to discuss what you are buying and why. Often people involved in the same supply chains have never even met – and the first added value you can deliver to the organization is to introduce them to each other.

Category analysis

Before we go into more detail, I think it might be worth just taking stock of where we are. There are many ways of cutting the information on your cost base and each has a role to play. At a *strategic level* there are your supply chains, each one of which is designed to deliver something important to your customers or your colleagues. We have already explored how important it is to make sure you understand the requirements you are attempting to satisfy and ensuring that all the assets at your disposal are optimized and aligned to meet those requirements in the most cost-effective way. At an *operational level* there are the goods and services that you buy and these can be categorized according to their general function. These goods and services might support many of your supply chains. An obvious example would be logistics. Logistics is a category of expenditure and can be broken down into lots of sub-categories such as air freight, road haulage, sea freight, courier services and so on. Typically most organizations will have 30–50 categories and up to 150 sub-categories.

The challenge that always faces you is how to optimize the sub-category at a general level while also making sure that the supply chains continue to receive the services they require to function. The only way to meet this challenge is to look at what you buy through both operational and strategic lenses. The strategic view will help to safeguard your value propositions and the operational one will make sure that you are leveraging the market and supply base effectively.

In this chapter we'll be looking at what you buy through this operational/category lens. The connection with the supply chain view is maintained because the first thing I am going to do is ask what the sub-category of expenditure is used for and how important it is to the business.

Category mapping

I am now going to introduce you to some techniques that can get the ball rolling and help your organization to assess the value and opportunity associated with the things you are buying and the motivations and attitudes of the suppliers that you are using. The tools are simple but can be very powerful, and their value lies not only in the output but also in the discussion they generate as you go through the process.

I know this is less a book for practitioners than it is a book to describe the art of procurement and its contribution to your organization, but I have always found that tools such as these shed such light onto the problems and opportunities of third-party expenditure that they are worth sharing with all stakeholders, regardless of their roles in any organization.

After such a fanfare, I am sure you are wondering what mystical things I am about to unveil, and you might be a little disappointed to find another two-by-two, in Figure 11.1. First let me describe what you are looking at and then I will give you some examples, starting with the two dimensions against which you will plot the sub-category, then the quadrants in the figure.

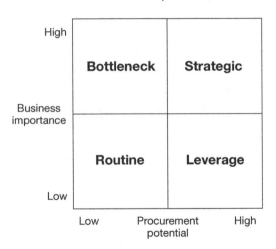

Figure 11.1   Category analysis matrix (Kraljic, 1983)

Business importance

This is your stakeholders' assessment of the importance to the business of the good or service you are buying. A good way of getting to the heart of this is to ask the question: 'What would the impact be of this good or service failing to do what it is supposed to do?' It is important that you future-proof answers to this, so some of the questions you ask must be pitched in such a way that forecast information can be teased out.

Procurement potential

This is your assessment of your organization's influence on the supply market for the good or service you are buying. Key to this are questions like: 'How many suppliers are there who can meet our requirements?' and, 'Do we spend a reasonable amount of money on acquiring this good or service?' The positioning on the grid is determined by the size and appetite of the supply market, the ease of switching suppliers, and your organization's leverage and attractiveness to the supply market. The challenge is in understanding the supplier market(s) that are capable of delivering the good or service under review as failure to do this effectively can deliver misleading results.

Bottleneck

If you don't spend much money on the good or service, or you are buying from a restricted or monopoly supplier, or the switching costs are very high – you are on the left-hand side of the bottom axis. If what you are buying is also business critical, the item will be plotted into the top left quadrant – which is the scariest place on this matrix and is labelled 'bottleneck'. Your strategy for bottleneck is always to move the item out of that quadrant, for example, by going for a standard specification instead of bespoke, or by using an agency (eg media buying) to increase your market clout.

Routine

If what you are buying is not business critical and you don't have much clout in the market then it should be plotted into the bottom left quadrant, which is labelled 'routine' and is likely to be something that you will only look at when you have nothing else to do. Once you do look at it then it is likely that you can save more money by streamlining your acquisition process than you can from shaving percentages off the acquisition price. For example, if you are buying a box of pencils then bear in mind that the typical cost of an order set (request, order, receipt and payment) is over US$70 (GBP £50).

Strategic

If you spend a reasonable amount of money on the good or service, have a healthy supply base and can switch suppliers relatively easily, then the service or good will be on the right-hand side of the bottom axis. If the good or service is also business critical then it should be plotted into the top right-hand quadrant and will be labelled 'strategic'. If you are determined to form a strategic alliance with a supplier, you should only consider it for a category that sits in this quadrant: it takes time, effort and commitment from both supplier and client to form a strategic alliance, and only things that are important to you and that you have some leverage over warrant this sort of attention.

Leverage

If the good or service is not important to the business but the supply market is healthy and your position is strong, it should be plotted into the bottom right-hand quadrant labelled 'leverage'. If you are going through this exercise to reduce costs then your eyes should light up with spinning £££ signs every time something falls into this classification because you spend a lot, the supply market is hot and it is easy to change supplier, which all means you can exploit the market without fear.

This is a pretty simple technique and you will have great conversations and a raised understanding of what you buy when you have gone through this exercise with your stakeholders. Now for some words of caution – things will move around the quadrants over time; suppliers will seek to move things around the quadrants and their ambition is always to be in the top half of the grid – because as already noted, when they are there you will care about them more!

Let's explore this in more detail and start by taking a look at innovation. When a good or service is new it is likely that you can only get it from one supplier, and if it is business critical then this means it is a bottleneck item.

As you will see from the arrow in Figure 11.2, over time and with careful management the innovative good or service being procured will move to the right. This could simply be because when you started out you were piloting it and now are spending much more on it. It could also be that there are more suppliers now able to offer the same or similar service. Ultimately the value of the innovation to your business could diminish as newer offerings come to market. If you are still buying the product at this time then it may become leverage or even routine. This happens especially in those fields that rely on innovation for market competitiveness (eg in oil and gas – the ability to find and extract more oil constantly drives the industry to seek out the cutting edge of reservoir mapping and directional drilling techniques).

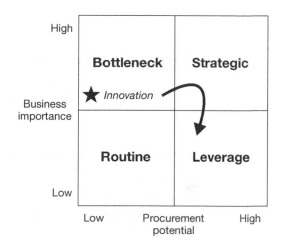

Figure 11.2 Category analysis of an innovative good

Another aspect that you need to be aware of is that services and systems are often a lot more important to the business than equipment or goods will be. As you can see in Figure 11.3, a personal computer (PC) is not important to the business: it is a piece of equipment that will at best be leverage if you buy lots of them, but could equally be routine. However, when you look at the supply chain in which the PC sits and reclassify the PC as part of your 'desktop services', suddenly it is a personal productivity tool, a repository of business critical information and it is right up there as strategic. Therefore when you are looking at the commodities you buy, you need to do this at various levels – by all means plot 'desktop services', but when you come to look at this in more detail break it down into the constituent parts (eg PC, software, helpdesk, peripherals) and plot these sub-components onto the grid too.

So in summary, this is an important and simple tool for you to use to analyse the goods and services you are buying and to identify those that you need to manage because they are important to you and those that will deliver cost-reduction opportunities with little business risk.

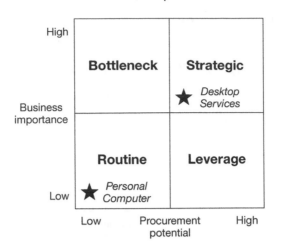

Figure 11.3 Category analysis of a service versus a good

What suppliers think of you

Now we know what is important to you, let's look at what your suppliers think about your business. It is very easy to assume that because a supplier is important to you, it feels the same way about you; unfortunately this isn't always the case. Figure 11.4 is a useful way of discussing and mapping your supplier's view of you. Let us look first at the dimensions against which we will plot our suppliers, then at the quadrants.

Account attractiveness

Measurement along this axis is usually rather subjective and to some extent will be driven by the alignment of your strategy with that of your suppliers. The sort of things that should be considered when plotting this include: if you are a 'blue chip' company, does working with you provide suppliers with a great reference that they can use to advantage with potential customers; as a pioneering organization you could be interested in piloting their products or collaborating on new ventures; or as a multinational you might be willing to take them into new territories.

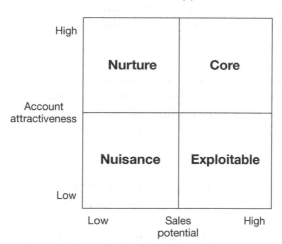

Figure 11.4 A supplier's analysis of your business

Sales potential

Against the horizontal axis you need to plot the suppliers' view of the value of your business to them. This is often determined by the revenue they receive (or think they could receive) from your account. This is both an absolute measure in respect of your spend with the suppliers as well as a relative measure in respect of their total revenue and other large clients.

I remember once talking to a supplier about this diagram and he said that the measure for his company, against both dimensions, was revenue. I found then and still find this remark to be rather bizarre because logically the more important measure to the supplier should surely be profitability. It is interesting, because as you seek to improve your relationship with the supplier and cut your costs then the relative importance of revenue and profit will be critical to the success of your negotiations. If the supplier is focused upon revenue from your account and you want to reduce your expenditure (but are happy to offer greater profitability) it could be difficult to get the supplier to understand the value of your proposition, and the dialogue is likely to stall. This is why it is important when selecting suppliers to assess the shortlist against not only objective but also subjective criteria – key amongst these will be cultural fit and strategic alignment. In teasing out the information it is important to discuss how success is measured in the sales force of the supplier and what the supplier's business objectives are (to become a million dollar revenue business is likely to be quite contrary to your ambitions).

Nurture

If the sales potential is low, but the account is attractive to the supplier, your business will be seen as something to nurture. As a client this is a good place to be as the supplier will be keen to build your business, retain your good regard and generally go the extra mile.

Core

If the sales potential is high and the account is attractive to the supplier, it will view your business as core to its success. As a client you can expect that the supplier will give your business board-level attention, which in turn should lead to good service, keen pricing and a focus on your strategic ambitions and its contribution to them. As I mentioned before, if the goods and services you are buying from it are strategic to your business then this is the relationship that you might want to treat as an alliance.

And now we get to the scary ones – especially if the goods and services you are buying from the supplier are important to you.

Nuisance

If your business is not valued either from a sales or account point of view, your custom will be seen as a nuisance. This means that the supplier will not be that bothered about winning or retaining your business. You can expect shoddy services, at least in your eyes, and a limited interest in responding to any tender you issue.

Exploitable

Worse still is if your sales potential is high but your account is not valued: in these circumstances you will be seen as exploitable. In this scenario the supplier will be happy to take your business but will not be particularly bothered about its quality or the delivered value for money. Your account is likely to be serviced by a slick-suited sales person rather than a service manager.

The more fragmented your expenditure is or the less you communicate your strategic ambition to your suppliers, the more likely you are to be in an uncomfortable position with them. Much of this is obviously fixable once you have done the analysis and studied the results. It might also start to answer some of the nagging doubts you had about the supplier's regard for your custom. Once you know the reasons, you can start to address them either by making yourself more attractive to the supplier or by finding a suitable alternative source for the goods or services that you need.

In summary

In this chapter we have looked at your spend and supply base through an operational lens. Where earlier chapters focused upon supply chains and how to ensure they meet the needs of your customers or colleagues, this operational analysis has allowed you to look holistically at what you buy and from whom. Evaluating your expenditure from this angle is critical in optimizing and leveraging your supply and its sources.

What you do with this information will be driven by the strategic imperatives of your business. If poor supplier engagement is creating problems, you could focus on securing better supplier performance by improving the suppliers' view of your business. Alternatively, if your bottom line performance could do with a boost then you could deliver cost reductions by better management and leverage of a specific category of expenditure. In the next chapter we are going to look at the sourcing process in more detail and how to optimize it to your benefit.

12 The secrets of sourcing

I hope that by now you have decided that I am onto something. You may have figured out what percentage of your cost base is actually with your suppliers. To give you a sleepless night you may have counted your suppliers – much more troublesome than sheep, trust me.

Now is the time to talk about some of the sourcing processes that you need to put in place to make sure that you are getting the most that you can out of your spend and critical suppliers. You may wonder why it has taken me until Chapter 12 to get to something that is so fundamental to procurement and, let's face it, is the place where many other books on procurement actually start. My excuse, and I think it's a good one, is that this book isn't really about the mechanics of procurement; it is more about its value proposition and strategic potential for your business.

In this chapter, therefore, I am going to briefly describe some of the critical things that you need to consider when you are deciding which suppliers' offers are most attractive and appropriate for your needs. This is a tale as much about avoiding the pitfalls as it is about seizing the value. The three areas I want to pick out deal with the process itself, your requirements and the supply market.

It's about more than the money

By now a heading like this from a procurement person like me shouldn't be such a surprise. We have already established that the success of your vision, business objectives and five-year plan will depend upon the way you manage all the assets that you have at your disposal. Key amongst these assets will be the external organizations with which you have a relationship; amongst the most important of these will be your suppliers. Therefore your success will be partly dependent upon those suppliers with which you will do business and particularly upon that subset of suppliers that deliver business critical goods and services to you and your customers.

This just emphasizes how important it is to have a well-defined sourcing approach that enables you to meet business needs, whether balancing short-term need with longer-term flexibility, cost reduction with added value, or delivery safeguards with innovation. As important as the process you use are the people that you involve in it. These supply decisions are too critical for any one person, even the CEO, to make on his or her own without first consulting others.

Level playing field

I know that many suppliers still don't really like having to deal with either a procurement department or a formal acquisition process but some, those I like to think of as enlightened, recognize that both can be valuable. They can be valuable because if there is a clear process there are likely to be agreed business requirements, an established business case and, most important, earmarked funding.

A clear process will also mean that *evaluation criteria* have been agreed before the process kicks off and will guide the selection process, helping to create a level playing field. Even the simplest of procurement processes will result in identifying a few criteria, such as quality, cost and corporate responsibility, which can be used to consistently evaluate offers. If the service being bought is complex or business critical, there will be other criteria such as cultural fit, shared values and some sort of strategic alignment. The criteria will be weighted and the supplier proposal will be scored against the criteria to inform the selection process. A level playing field means that suppliers and their solutions will be evaluated against a mix of objective and subjective criteria.

What has been proved over and over to me is that whatever preconceptions stakeholders arrive with, a robust procurement process will help get to the right answer for the business and create buy-in to the chosen solution – which really helps when implementation starts. Ultimately, while no one likes to be told they have been unsuccessful, detailed feedback on the reasons for failure to win work is hugely powerful, and I would encourage all suppliers to ensure they are not fed any platitudes and really dig deep to fully understand the reasons.

Reciprocity

This leads me nicely to the last thing I want to explore under this heading – the lure and pitfalls of creating complex relationships when you are both a supplier to and a customer of another organization. Right at the beginning of this book we recognized that in today's complex world very few companies have straightforward relationships with each other. In certain industries, eg financial services, automotive or energy, it is very likely that you will have suppliers that are also customers; it is equally likely that you will have suppliers that you partly own. Regulation will ensure that for some of these relationships, you operate Chinese Walls and this is good. For all other relationships I suggest that the golden rule is that each of the business relationships makes sense in its own right.

If you are awarding a contract, the supplier you give the business to must be the right one for your organization. Similarly, if you are thinking about investing in a company that is also a supplier to you, that investment must stand on its own merits. If all things are equal and the choice is down to two suppliers, then the one you have a deeper relationship with might win the day. This is as close to the proverbial win-win as you are likely to get.

Anything more convoluted than this could be a commercial minefield. If you award business because your company part-owns the supplier, you are potentially propping up a supplier that doesn't warrant it, and just imagine what happens next if your organization decides to dispose of its holding – you could be tied into a poor-quality relationship for years.

Requirements

You need to know what you need. No, I'm not going to go over old ground. I am well aware that you may think that several of the earlier chapters in this book have done this topic to death. But this is where the rubber really hits the road. You have come up with your needs statement, your functional specification and your scope of supply – those elements that clearly articulate what you and your customers will value from the thing you are making or buying.

You must also understand your current total costs. You need to know this because if you are going to make the right decisions when you come to evaluate alternative sources of supply you must account for all the costs associated with your proposed solution and compare them with your current total costs. One of the greatest challenges of working in global supply markets is making sure that you are comparing apples with apples when you evaluate them. Figure 12.1 provides a good example of the sort of factors that need to be taken into consideration. As you will see from the illustration, we have gone out into the market with the specification of the component that we want to buy. By going to manufacturers in the emerging markets of the Far East, it looks like we have found a great source of supply that will save us 15 per cent on the price paid to the incumbent supplier. So far so good. However, the picture changes somewhat when we start to add the costs associated with logistics (we now need to transport it half-way around the world), inventory (even if we can leave the ownership with the supplier while in transit, we need to carry higher levels of both stock and emergency buffer stock because the inventory lead time is greater), and extra layers of quality control and higher stock holdings (which in turn increase our risk of obsolescence). In my example this gets us to a neutral cost position. If you go on to factor in additional costs (albeit shared) of local procurement and quality assurance resources, this great deal doesn't look so irresistible any more.

As illustrated in Figure 12.1, some of the elements of total costs that can be overlooked are longer transportation times (especially if sea freighting), which mean that inventory and safety stocks might need to increase, the need to have local offices to manage the supply base, and currency hedges or other risk management factors. Another element that needs to be taken into account is the sheer cost of switching supplier. Sometimes the supplier is so embedded into a supply chain that the cost of changing becomes prohibitive. You only need to look at some of the 'hole in the wall' operations (effectively the co-location of key suppliers with their key customer) of some of the automotive operations to see that this might be an issue. For example, synchronous delivery operations such as those conducted at the Nissan plant in the North East of England have many advantages. Under synchronous delivery, a signal is sent from the assembly

Figure 12.1 Example of total cost of ownership study

line that in a matter of hours the next car down the line is going to be orange. This notification allows the seat supplier to arrange for four seats with appropriate trim to be delivered from the supplier site to the exact point in the line where these seats can be bolted into place. I suggest that in this instance the switching cost associated with the displacement of the incumbent supplier, the establishment of the new supplier and the disruption this could cause to the production line would be disproportionate to any unit cost reduction.

Unfortunately, high switching costs don't always relate to careful sourcing decisions such as those in the case of Nissan. Sometimes they are the by-product of very old sourcing initiatives that have been ill-thought through. Even some of these hole-in-the-wall automotive operations will fall into this category. For example, co-location can mean the manufacturer imposing its inherent cost base on its supplier because of its geographic location and the conditions of the labour market. If you remember from Chapter 11, high switching costs can mean plotting the category into 'bottleneck' and recognizing the incumbent supplier as the only viable source of supply.

Supply market knowledge

Once you have defined the supply market(s) then you need good market intelligence. Just because you picked a certain supplier last time around doesn't mean that it is a shoo-in now. The market might be changing: there could be new technical innovations or market entrants that are capable, given the chance, of delivering a step-change in productivity or customer satisfaction. Your current supplier might have its hands full with a new client it is on-boarding and doesn't have time for you. Or it might have financial challenges that are going to mean that service, quality or, more worryingly, supply continuity are going to be threatened. There might be suppliers you have never heard of emerging in new geographies with cost-advantaged capabilities that incumbent suppliers cannot match. You need all this information and more to even get to your long list of potential suppliers.

I have always found Michael E Porter's five competitive forces that he created to determine industry profitability work very well when you are trying to figure out the potential supply market to meet your need. Just to remind you, Porter (1985) states that there are five competitive forces at work in any industry. These are:

existing competition, the power of both buyers and suppliers in the market, the threat of substitutes, and barriers to new entrants. What I particularly like about Porter's model is that it takes account of substitutes and new entrants. If I were looking at business travel I would include video and telephone conferencing as potential substitutes to the *need* of business travel, and their providers as new entrants alongside the more traditional travel companies. This obviously assumes that the need is something along the lines of: 'To facilitate effective communication within and outside the company to achieve the business objectives of sales, service, management and culture.'

Suppliers that differentiate

At some point and perhaps from day one, to avoid being commoditized or disintermediated by your customers, you will seek to differentiate your brand and your solution. This is obviously great stuff. What you might not have given much thought to is that your suppliers, in order to avoid being commoditized by you, will seek to differentiate their brand and their solutions too. The most common way in which suppliers have differentiated themselves is by delivering higher value, better service and greater innovation to their corporate customers. More recently, some suppliers have decided that this isn't enough or isn't delivering what they want, and have sought to differentiate themselves directly with the customers of their corporate client.

The most famous, and certainly the most successful, example of this is Intel when it worked to create a brand that was recognized by the public (effectively by its customers' customers). Brought to life by its marketing campaign at a time when 'ingredient branding' was a relatively new concept, Intel's logo and its accompanying catchy jingle were soon widely known.

One of the best and most enduring ways to capture the public's attention is to turn your brand into a verb. I always 'Hoover the house' and 'Google a fact' and while I haven't quite got around to 'Twittering', that probably says more about me that it does about Twitter. 'Intel Inside' is a pretty good equivalent of this and a shrewd marketing tactic. In the market for personal computers, which has itself become heavily commoditized, what better way of safeguarding your market share and margin than by making the customers of your customers actively seek out your components in the products they want to buy? Who can watch the adverts for Intel's corporate customers' computer ads and not think of Intel? What Intel did very smartly is ensure that customers, even fairly ignorant customers (and I include myself amongst them), know that 'Intel Inside' means quality and faster processing. And don't you think that, because these manufacturers and Intel are locked in such an overt and symbiotic relationship, negotiations on target cost are just going to that bit more difficult for the manufacturers?

Suppliers that disintermediate

Given the opportunity, your suppliers might also attempt to disintermediate you from your own supply chain and customer base. Look at the airlines' websites and high street travel agencies to recognize the potential for this. The travel agents used to be the airlines' key business conduit to the passengers; now some of the low-cost airlines won't even deal with travel agents but insist on direct customer relationships with their passengers through their websites.

Another example is insurance, as providers bypass insurance brokers to establish direct relationships with the insured. What is interesting about this is the rise of online comparison websites that are effectively recreating the broker's role, albeit through the web. Disintermediation is intended to cut out the middle man and no one can argue that the web has made a lot more information universally available and searchable. However, the limited occurrence of disintermediation does make one realize that information overload brings its own intermediation opportunities.

All that said, when you are constructing your supply chain, a good test of your value proposition is whether or not someone could do it without you. If you hold the patents, intellectual property rights or valued brand in the supply chain – probably not; otherwise, maybe.

Supply market distortion

We have already established that the health and well-being of your company is inextricably linked to that of the key suppliers you work with. This should force your company to look at both the short- and long-term implications of your actions for the supply markets and suppliers you work with. Unfortunately, the longer-term implications are something that many organizations are unwilling or unable to grapple with.

When an organization is facing squeezed margins and tough competition, it is obviously important that it can meet these short-term challenges and basically live to fight another day. Compound this with the fact that many key decision makers in the organization are likely to have a 12-month performance, appraisal and reward horizon, and it is easy to see how all these factors encourage us to make short- or medium-term decisions and leave longer-term issues for the longer term.

If we are faced with supply choices that put all our eggs into the best basket today, even recognizing that this is likely to damage the health of the supply market and the competitiveness of its participants in the longer term, many of us are likely to take the short-term view. At best some of us will award small pieces of business to emerging companies or the also-rans, but this is all too often more of a gesture than a move of substance.

All of this is understandable. However, if we turn around in five years and complain because there is no genuine competition in the market, that the incumbent suppliers have become complacent and we have no leverage in the face of near-monopoly suppliers, let's just remember that we share the blame for this.

Cost advantaged supply

One of the biggest challenges facing companies now is to understand the cost structure of the markets we buy from, so that we know when we are tapping into a cost advantaged supplier and when the supplier is slashing its margins and 'buying the business'. Both of these situations can be all right – provided that we know what is going on. Who doesn't love the occasional loss-leader, the special offer that is there to hook us in? However, when times are tough and finance is tight, too many loss-leader contracts can mean danger to both the supplier and our supply. Therefore we need to understand the cost structure of the good or service we are buying and the cost advantage of the suppliers that provide it.

Table 12.1 Product/service cost structure

Element	Cost drivers
Labour	Utilization rates Productivity Labour costs
Raw materials	Quality Leverage Vertical integration Substitutes
Transport	Bulk and weight Distance
Energy	Process efficiency Unit cost

Table 12.1 shows us some of the bigger elements that will make up the costs of the good or service, such as labour, raw materials, transport and energy. For example, the cost structure of a consultant is likely to be predominantly labour-related and the cost drivers will be utilization (the higher the utilization rate the lower the unit cost); labour cost (the fully loaded cost of the individual – salary and overheads); and productivity (if the consultant can reuse knowledge on your engagement it can be completed faster and to higher quality). Alternatively, if the product is milled steel, the main costs will be raw materials, energy and transport, and the cost drivers will be the availability and cost of the raw materials (quality required and leverage capability of the supplier); transport (distance from both its source and destination and mode required); and energy (efficiency of the plant and the manufacturing process).

Once you have identified the cost profile of the good or service, you can start to identify suppliers that can offer genuine cost advantages. For example, the milled steel manufacturer that is in close proximity to the source of its raw materials and its customer market will be able to offer lower costs than a manufacturer in a remote location with access to lower cost labour. This is because in this example, transport costs represent a much higher percentage of the cost of its production than labour does. This is a simple example of a more complex exercise, the completion of which will help you to distinguish between suppliers that are buying your business and those that are sharing the benefits of their cost-beneficial supply chain.

If we understand the cost structure of our suppliers we can also start to re-engineer our relationship with the suppliers to reduce the costs for us and for them. This is covered in more detail in Chapter 19. But to whet your appetite: if you knew that a systems integrator (ie those companies that will implement complex IT systems into your business and integrate them with existing applications) typically spends over 25 per cent of its operating costs on bidding for work (remember the tender process for such pieces of work is often more than 12 months and can cost millions) then you might think about re-engineering your contracting process if the supplier will share the process savings with you.

Size matters, but be careful what you measure

Just because you are the biggest company in the world doesn't mean that when you are looking for a suitable supplier you should only look at the biggest companies in the supply market. One thing I have noticed as everything ostensibly becomes global is just how much actually remains local and even parochial. While it is true that suppliers will often have global, regional and national accounts, day-to-day management will almost always be local, with the customer services director based in the same city as the main client contacts.

The key to me seems to be not so much how large or global you are as an organization, but how significant and geographically spread your needs are. In this way, an international roll-out of a new computer system will probably require an international supplier capable of providing a consistent and uniform solution globally, whereas a marketing campaign for China will need high levels of local content. In all this the important factor is the international or local nature of your requirements and not the international or local nature of either your organization or the supply market.

Therefore when you are assembling your supplier shortlist, you should evaluate their capabilities against your requirements to determine how appropriate their geography and scale are. If you select a supplier because it is your equivalent in its market (you are number one and so is it), you could end up being unimportant to the supplier because while overall you are large, your business needs are too small to be of interest to it. On the other hand, beware the temptation to give your custom to a smaller organization if it means that you become more than a third of its business volume. While it might be nice to know that you are the supplier's most important customer, it becomes very uncomfortable if, for whatever reason, you want to move to a new supplier. It can also be very tempting to give the supplier more business because you want to become more important to it (perhaps you are suffering from lack of attention on a critical service). Once again I advise caution – you must make sure that the bundle of business makes sense to both of you from the get-go.

In summary

This chapter has been a smorgasbord of some of the things you will want to consider when making your sourcing decisions. Most particularly, I picked out items associated with specification of requirements, the procurement process and characteristics and consideration of supply. Sourcing decisions are key to the success of your supply chain and therefore a robust process involving the right stakeholders and evaluating the right elements of both needs and capability, is a vital step in getting off to a great start and achieving the Nirvana-like state of getting it right first time.

13 Sharing the pain in hard times

Don't be a shock absorber

Years ago I worked as a consultant for a provider of equipment and infrastructure to the mobile communications sector. The company had enjoyed years of unprecedented growth and plenty, its market share was large, 3G technology was on the horizon with untold opportunities, and the phrase 'cost management' was a genuine oxymoron. My role and that of anyone trying to improve the company's approach to third-party spend was a nightmare. I remember being told, 'If my new hire wants a Porsche, she gets a Porsche!' He wasn't talking about me by the way.

Anyone who remembers the introduction of 3G technology in Europe and the bidding wars for licences, particularly in the United Kingdom, Germany and Italy, knows very well what happened next – the bubble burst. The companies had taken on huge debt to pay for the licences; the telecoms industry was regarded as synonymous with high tech and dot com, and the dot com bubble had well and truly burst. Suddenly the company I was working for was under huge pressure and cost management, needless to say, became a key company strategy.

Interestingly, when the company decided to introduce measures to substantially reduce its costs, its initial port of call was internal expenditure, most particularly to reduce the number of employees it had. The company actually took advantage of the crisis to drive through changes that senior management had been keen to do for some time. One of these initiatives was to remove the back office processes that sat in every business unit in every country across the world and create regional shared service centres. This was a very laudable and appropriate thing to do and has continued to deliver value ever since. Eventually and to my mind rather late in the day, the company turned its attention to its third-party expenditure and supply base. What I thought was fascinating was the genuine but misplaced desire of the company to absorb the bad times in the same way it had, presumably, enjoyed the good. Therefore it had looked internally before it had looked externally for cost reduction opportunities.

It was then that I coined the phrase, 'Don't be a shock absorber.' The market was tight and many customers could no longer pay for routine services. This effectively shrank the revenues that the company had always been able to rely on. Crazy prices had been paid for unprofitable market share and margins were quickly eroding. Despite this desperate plight, the majority of people I spoke to at all levels in the business thought that they just had to weather the bad times. Needless to say, I was trying to get them to share the pain with their suppliers.

If you think that I was being mean, then let me tell you that these suppliers had been getting equally fat during the good times and I was doing them a favour by putting them on a diet! Of course I wasn't just telling them to reduce their prices, though I would always recommend that you get to bedrock pricing before starting to do anything fancier. I was trying to help the suppliers to reduce their costs in order to reduce their prices. Before you give me the Nobel Peace Prize for such altruism, I have to confess that taking cost out rather than an unending process of slashing prices and margin is actually the only way to get to real sustainable improvement, which is what we should all be aiming to achieve.

In this chapter we will explore how to get going when the going gets tough and how to convince the organization that third-party supplier and cost management have a major role to play in turnaround situations. We will then discuss how to make sure that when the situation, whether specific to the company, the industry or the economy, improves, you don't end up back at square one.

When the going gets tough

Sometimes a crisis of some sort is exactly what an organization needs to wake up to the opportunities presented by better management of its third-party spend. When the top team discover that fundamental change is imperative, it provides the focus required to make it happen. Cost reduction programmes require strong sponsorship from the top.

Any organization that turns the cost reduction lens on only its internal costs is going to leave lots of value on the table. You only need to look at the balance sheet to recognize this. As mentioned before, traditional manufacturing industries such as automotive will have third-party spend that represents 80 per cent or more of their total cost base. Even service industries are now likely to have suppliers representing 50 per cent of their cost base. For the oil majors such as Shell and Exxon Mobil, whose third-party spend is a small percentage of their overall cost base (largely because of the oil and gas itself), it is still going to be several tens of billions of dollars every year. Therefore any company that doesn't look at its external as well as internal costs is going to miss an opportunity. And because it is important to focus on sustainable cost health for the organization, costs should no longer be segregated along the lines of internal and external – they should be oriented towards the processes and supply chains they support. Allocating your attention along such artificial lines is rather like trying to optimize a function in isolation from the processes it supports. It is easy to improve to a point but will inhibit more trans-formational opportunities.

Even companies that have been recognized as good at procurement can get a real shot in the arm in tough times. I say this because in most companies there are usually some areas that will not have been a focus of attention but which can deliver value. Sometimes these initiatives have been assessed as delivering only marginal returns on the effort required; others are just not very palatable. For example, I don't think I have ever worked in an organization or an industry that didn't have some sacred cows – by that I mean areas of expenditure that were never going to be managed proactively or professionally. In the oil and gas industry, the exploration team often have lots of them, like the relationships that they believe are key to their success in finding oil and gas reserves and therefore must not be sullied by commercialism. In the health sector, it has often been those items required for surgical procedures (partly due to high switching costs) or others items needed by consultants and doctors.

In many companies, regardless of sector, spend on marketing would be one such area, though 'the times they are a-changing'. I was particularly interested to hear Sir Martin Sorrell, CEO of WPP Group, which is one of the largest global advertising companies, in June 2009 blaming procurement departments in customer organizations for depressing margins (Bradshaw, 2009). I find that especially interesting as his company has obviously woken up to the value that can be delivered to its own organization through better procurement. In the same reporting period, the WPP board said in its mid-year trading statement that one of its key strategies for WPP was to leverage the group's buying power on behalf of its clients (WPP, 2009).

When there is a crisis or something else that means that a business needs to take a long, hard look at itself, it is often worth looking at these historically no-go areas. This is partly because there is likely to be more appetite from the board to tackle these thorny subjects and partly because the benefits are likely to be more substantial as they haven't necessarily been subject to strong commercial scrutiny. This doesn't mean that I am suggesting that the procurement department should be unleashed like marauding hordes on these sacrosanct areas of expenditure. Instead, whatever the door opener has been, I consider it a real opportunity to demonstrate that commercialism and value for money are mutually inclusive. With good procurement the users will still get the best services from their suppliers, but now they will also have contracts that protect the interests of the buying organization, with pricing structures and service levels that reward the supplier for delivering against the requirements of the organization. This is one way in which you can deliver and balance both short- and long-term value.

Another area that is often neglected in many companies is indirect spend – that part of your spend that doesn't go into the goods and services that you sell to clients and customers. Even many manufacturers ignore this – they work very hard on their direct spend and totally ignore the costs in the back office. The great thing about indirect spend is that much of it is not business critical to your organization and, if you think back to Chapter 11 where we plotted spend against the axis of business importance and procurement potential, you will recall that non-business critical spend can be quite a cash cow for saving money for your organization. You can be quite aggressive in striking deals for these goods and services in the knowledge that if you get it wrong you can painlessly move to another supplier and the business will not suffer. One of the reasons that indirect spend is often not as well managed commercially as direct spend is that it includes some tricky categories, such as travel and consultancy. These are not strategic to the business but the business can get emotional about them. As such some of the categories in your indirect spend are likely to be sacred cows. So once again there is a great opportunity when times are tough to overcome these emotional barriers and demonstrate that good commercial practices can deliver value on a number of fronts.

When the going gets very, very tough

Sometimes the environment is so tough and the burning platform so hot, that you have to take cost out very quickly. Once again, better management of third-party spend can come to the rescue. If you have cash flow problems, you might be able to renegotiate payment terms with some suppliers that aren't feeling the same pain as you. This could help you manage your cash conversion cycle (the time from paying for the creation of your product or service to receiving payment for it). Obviously, the shorter the cycle the better, and it can be helped by securing better terms from your suppliers. A rather extreme example is when Boeing negotiated an agreement with the suppliers involved in the new 787 Dreamliner that they wouldn't be paid until the aircraft was delivered. As the plane is in development this could be years away; however, recent delays to the launch date have caused Boeing to revisit these terms with some suppliers (Blackwell, 2009).

At the other extreme you could introduce purchasing cards that pay your suppliers within a few days but give you two months' credit – this is much more of a win-win for both you and your suppliers. Another opportunity is where customers increase their payment days but through finance companies, and banks offer online factoring services such that the supplier can selectively seek early payment of its invoices for a reduction in the face value of the invoice.

In these situations, some companies ask their suppliers for radical cost reductions. In recent years the automotive industry has done this rather regularly, and it is a factor in the collapse of their global automotive suppliers' average earnings before interest and tax (EBIT) by about half between 2007 and 2008 (Roland Berger, 2009). Obviously the relationships between the automotive companies and their suppliers are rather symbiotic – perhaps too much so. However, while this type of action is an option, I think it is always preferable to give something of value to the supplier in return, such as more business, longer contracts, different payment terms or access to strategic markets. I prefer this path for a variety of reasons, the primary one being that while you do have a relationship with your suppliers it is a commercial not an emotional one. A good question to ask yourself is, if the situations were reversed, how much would I be willing to do for our beleaguered supplier? The answer might help you assess what you can reasonably ask of your suppliers now while still maintaining reasonable, balanced relations with them in the longer term.

Getting your own house in order

A burning platform can enable you to tackle the unthinkable. If your organization continues to do things the way it always has then cost reduction has a role, but it is likely to be marginal. If your organization is willing to do things radically differently then cost reduction can be huge. After all, taking 10 per cent off the cost of something has much less impact than eliminating 80 per cent of the demand for it.

I have already mentioned that one of the things you can do is look at areas that historically you haven't managed particularly commercially. This may be because the pay-back seemed small, or because the stakeholders were too precious. But there are other things you can do too. You can challenge the demand for and the specification of the things you are buying: is the policy appropriate, who needs to use it and how is the demand authorized? Obvious areas of focus include travel, consultants, temporary resources, office accommodation, IT equipment and photocopiers. When I was working for the mobile phone operator, we established that if the entire photocopier estate were used continuously for just a few hours it would accommodate an entire year's worth of printing requirements – in other words, the company had far too many copiers for the demand and reducing the estate was an obvious opportunity.

Sometimes you find that the contracts agreed between you and your suppliers mean that the speed at which you can change direction and reduce demand is very slow. This is something you should think about when setting contracts in the first place – never commit to volumes unless you are absolutely sure that you will need them, and ideally never commit to volumes full stop. It is amazing how many buyers are really sure that they need something for certain but within months the company strategy has changed, customers have turned against the solution or a merger or takeover happens. The only sure thing in procurement is the contract and therefore, all things being equal, make sure there is sufficient flexibility in it – especially in respect of commitments to volume, which are to be avoided ideally or carefully stress-tested if necessary.

In summary

The journey through both good and bad times is taken hand-in-hand with your suppliers. When times become more challenging for you, your first instinct should be to look at all your direct costs and take the opportunity to challenge demand and the sacred cows of spend across the organization. You should encourage your suppliers to help, ideally by working with you to cut costs out of the supply chain – costs that won't come back when the good times do.

14 Avoiding the perils of outsourcing

Be careful of getting what you wish for

I worked as a consultant to a multinational several years ago and when I arrived everyone, from the CEO down, said to me, 'If you do one thing while you are here, you must change the supplier of our data centre outsourcing. They provide a dreadful service and are ripping us off.' I am going to share with you more of this story during this chapter, but suffice to say that I ended up doing nothing of the sort and yet my client was delighted with the solution.

We have talked a lot in this book about the importance of getting things right first time and about really understanding what you need and value. All along I have been emphasizing the fact that you need to do both long before you start talking to potential suppliers. Once you have selected your supplier, it is equally important that you create a contract that rewards the supplier for doing what you value, and that you establish a team that will manage the relationship with the supplier and ensure that you are getting value for what you are paying for.

If any of these elements is not in place it is likely that the relationship between client and supplier will break down. And if this happens, it is quite natural that the client will decide that the relationship is unsupportable and will seek to break the contract and find an alternative provider. Unfortunately, and I am sure you can see the truth of this, even if the client manages to get out of the contract and the relationship, finds another supplier and enters a new contract, the odds are that, after the inevitable honeymoon period, the client and its new supplier will be unhappy with each other. Albert Einstein defined insanity as 'doing the same thing over and over again and expecting different results'.

In this chapter we are going to explore a process you can follow if you do find yourself in relationships and contracts which, for whatever reason, do not meet your expectations. By the way, every good book has to have a quote from Albert Einstein – this book must be very good as it now has at least two.

Back to the multinational

Pretty soon after arriving at the multinational, someone gave me the contract. It was actually leather-bound (I wouldn't recommend that by the way), in a very small typeface and roughly the length of the entire works of Shakespeare. What I discovered was that the first problem with the relationship was the contract. It was out of date – while the contract wasn't particularly old it hadn't been future-proofed. Instead it had been created to cover only the immediate requirements of the organization, which at the time it was created had been the provision of mainframe services. Needless to say, technology had moved on, systems had been replaced and the growth area in the data centres was mid-range computing.

The next issue with the contract was that it didn't encourage the data centre provider to deliver the services that were of value to the client. For example, the provider was paid by MIPS (millions of instructions per second) and DASD (directly addressable storage device), which are both technical terms used to measure the processing power and amount of data storage – two measures of cost for the data centre service provider. Essentially these measures meant that the more capacity there was in the data centre (regardless of its use) the more the supplier got paid. There was no incentive therefore for the provider to rationalize the hardware or to better utilize the assets – in fact it wouldn't be much of an exaggeration to say that every new application got its own server. The combination of the payment mechanism and the proliferation of hardware meant that the costs to the business units went up and yet the reason for this, the cause and effect, was not obvious to budget holders.

All these problems with the contract were compounded by the way the relationship was managed. This only became apparent when I ran a supply chain analysis workshop with a team of people who were involved with the supplier and throughout the supply chain. When the company had outsourced its IT infrastructure and data centre requirements it had transferred most of its staff to the supplier and had decided not to retain any senior people who understood the services that the organization would now draw down from its outsource provider. This had lots of implications, one of the key ones being that effectively the company was not an 'intelligent buyer' of IT infrastructure services.

The process that had been put in place to manage the introduction of new system requirements into the data centre was complicated. A requisition was raised by the business detailing the application that was to be implemented or upgraded. This was passed to the service provider which then determined (largely independently) the additional capacity required. As I've already mentioned, there was no incentive for the provider to optimize the environment and therefore this new requirement almost inevitably led to new hardware being commissioned. As far as the business was concerned there was no correlation between the systems being supported in the data centre and the MIPs and DASD-based costs that were then invoiced. The costs and frustrations just mounted.

There was no formal supplier or contract management team in the company managing the relationship with the service provider and no one who understood the terms of the contract or who could make sense of the charges. Because there were no IT-savvy people left in the multinational, or at least none that were involved in managing the service delivery of the contract, there was no one who was trying to improve the relationship or manage the costs.

The good news was that the fundamentals of the service were robust and the reliability of the infrastructure was very high and well within agreed service levels. This meant that the service provider was good at its job and capable of meeting the needs of the organization.

Once we had completed the investigation of the contract and the analysis of the supply chain, we had a clear understanding of the drivers of cost associated with the service and also an understanding of how to increase the value that could be delivered to the business.

Getting to a relationship that worked

Supply chain analysis, using a cross-functional team, is a powerful technique that very quickly provides an end-to-end view of the supply chain, its cost and value drivers. It also encourages the team to identify hypotheses about the ways in which the supply chain could be improved.

The hypotheses that we decided were worth pursuing included the creation of an intelligent buyer role and supplier management function within the company to manage the contract; the introduction of key changes to the contract that encouraged the provider to optimize the utilization of, and ultimately support the rationalization of, the equipment in the data centres; modified pricing policies that forecast for the business the likely cost of the support for its new applications and introduced a more transparent billing process, both of which facilitated better cost management by the business; and finally developed a gainshare arrangement that promoted the optimization of the IT infrastructure and services provided through the data centres, including reuse strategies and retirement of redundant equipment. This effectively describes the new arrangements that we negotiated on behalf of the company with its existing service provider. The total cost of the service reduced by over 5 per cent, the relationship improved and the two organizations started to work together in the pursuit of mutually beneficial strategies. The issues that needed to be, and were, resolved through this approach related to the contract, reward mechanism and ultimately the relationship between the two organizations.

Had we done what the company thought it needed and selected a new service provider, it is likely that at some point the relationship would have foundered and the multinational would have found itself back at square one. This is why this chapter is called 'Be careful of getting what you wish for' and why Einstein isn't recognized as a genius for nothing.

15 Corporate responsibility

Good corporate citizenship

How can an organization claim to be a good corporate citizen without extending its responsibilities into its supply chains? The simple answer is that it cannot. Corporate responsibility in its widest sense means the consistent application of ethical and sustainable business principles and as such must expand to cover the whole supply chain and its suppliers. Failure to live up to customer expectations of corporate responsibility is one of the most damaging things an organization can do to its brand. Indeed, strong corporate responsibility is a key enabler to enhancing and, at the very least, sustaining brand and customer relationships. A strong sense of corporate responsibility is one of the must-have characteristics that many graduates look for when determining which company they might want to work for.

By way of example therefore, it is interesting when you consider that most carbon reduction targets are inwardly focused: they measure the property and personnel footprints in terms of energy consumption of buildings such as offices, manufacturing plants and data centres, travel and miscellaneous elements such as printing and photo-copying. They don't consider the demands you place upon your suppliers.

Going back to our original premise that between 20 and 80 per cent of your direct costs are through your suppliers, to change the lens when it comes to corporate responsibility seems, at best, rather naïve. In fairness, some of the statistics that companies measure do include suppliers. For example, your carbon footprint is still measured for property and transport where you may not own the building or the manufacturing plant, and you are almost certain not to own the railways, aeroplanes, vans and cars you utilize. However, other things such as the transport and distribution of materials and supplies and contract manufacturing are going to remain on the environmental scorecard of your suppliers.

If your organization is truly committed to its corporate responsibilities then you need to push out into your supply base. The good news is that there are many ways of doing this and it doesn't need to cost you or the Earth! In this chapter we are going to explore how to use your power responsibly, expand your corporate values across your supply chains and reward the services and actions you value.

Defining corporate responsibility

Corporate responsibility covers a variety of things – ethics, environment, sustainability, equality and fairness. It is something that in recent years has come to the forefront of public consciousness and has become a must-have or hygiene factor for most if not all organizations. For example, in 2008, Fairtrade-certified worldwide sales were almost €3 billion and had increased 20 per cent on the previous year. Across North America and Europe, Fairtrade goods make up between 1 and 20 per cent of the product markets in which they operate (Fairtrade, 2009). What this seems to demonstrate is that, all things being equal, consumers are willing to seek out Fairtrade-certified products.

I have used the term 'all things being equal' very deliberately because I think that one of the dilemmas businesses face is the premium that consumers are willing and able to pay for social and environmentally responsible supply. While not directly synonymous, I think the impact of the economic downturn in 2008–2010 on the organic food market and the increasing prominence of very cheap clothing retailers puts a significant question mark on consumers' willingness to do without something rather than risk exploiting either the environment or a labour force. It is probably easier for a company in a growing market to set out and live up to its corporate responsibility ambitions. When markets shrink and price becomes the biggest differentiator, it becomes more difficult but, potentially, no less important.

What is different is the hubris with which companies embrace the ethos. I still believe that corporate responsibility is important.

However, I think that it has been moving in the last few years from a shiny new buzz phrase to something that is more meaningful and measured. I consider it is a little bit like the dot com phenomenon that bloomed in the 1990s and burst so spectacularly in 2001, to be followed by an internet economy that is relentlessly changing our world.

One of the challenges that must be overcome as we move inexorably forward in the corporate responsibility journey is the fact that, especially when assessing the environmental impact of certain actions, the answers are often far from black and white. For example, when you buy copier paper is there less environmental damage from recycled paper or from paper created from sustainable woodland? When you install hand-drying facilities in facilities on your premises are you better using paper towels, flannel towels or electric hand-driers? Straight answers to these complex questions will help a lot.

Differentiating corporate responsibility

It is interesting how similar a lot of companies' corporate responsibility statements are, despite the fact that they operate in different industries. There are obviously common elements such as equality and diversity, but there should also be some differences. A statement on the environment by an oil company is much more important and profound than one made by a bank. Similarly, a statement on treating customers fairly in a bank is more meaningful than it would be in mining company whose customers are most likely to be metal traders.

Establishing meaningful and differentiated elements of one's corporate responsibility agenda is the key to making it count with stakeholders, whether they are shareholders, employees, suppliers or customers. It also helps turn rhetoric into practice, as meaningful and heartfelt measures are more likely to result in concrete and measurable activities.

Embedding corporate responsibility

Once the elements of your corporate responsibility agenda have been agreed and published it is important to mobilize your organization to support it. And when you are mobilizing your organization, don't forget to engage your key suppliers.

Embedding your corporate responsibility agenda is fundamental to putting your signature on your supply chain. When you mobilize your suppliers and they mobilize their suppliers and so on, it is very important to make sure everyone understands what you expect not only in terms of output but also of acceptability. It would be tragic on many fronts if any of your suppliers, even inadvertently, betrayed your ethos and your brand.

A good place to start is at the beginning – and this isn't as facetious a statement as it probably sounds. When you are considering companies to become part of your supply chain, it really helps if you assess their corporate responsibility approach and track record before you even think about putting them on your shortlist. You can and should do this when you are assessing the strategic alignment and cultural fit of potential suppliers to your organization. While these are rather subjective criteria, these elements of your assessment can be as important as their technical capability.

Where the supply chain or the goods and services you need to acquire are particularly sensitive to elements of your corporate responsibility agenda, it is appropriate to dig more deeply. For example, if you are buying office furniture you will want to ensure that the timber sources are sustainable and do not use endangered trees from fragile environments. Similarly, if you are buying clothing from emerging markets, the employment and labour practices of the manufacturers become very important.

More challenging, but still achievable, will be the checks that your potential suppliers need to undertake within their own supply chains. It is not good enough to perform due diligence only on the first tier of your suppliers and, while you might not do it yourself, it has to be visibly done.

Once you have made your supplier selection, it is important to reflect the key elements of your corporate responsibility agenda in the contract in the same way that you would expect your contract to reflect compliance with your data security and other company policies. Where material, this should include physical or at least desktop auditing to ensure ongoing conformance. I have seen this done to good effect in the UK public sector, where in some cases the recognized labour unions were invited to visit the factories in China to ensure that practices were appropriate. This had the added benefit of gaining support from yet another stakeholder group to the appropriateness of the contract and provided the opportunity to influence positively the supplier's working conditions.

A supply chain view

When an organization sets its environmental targets they are often very inwardly focused. For example, a company will assess its carbon footprint and establish a reduction target against it. However, to deliver a step change in performance it can be better to look at and set targets for your key supply chains. In the same way that you would re-engineer your supply chain to make it more cost-effective or time responsive, you can do so for environmental effectiveness. What is interesting is how much a reduction in your carbon emissions can make commercial sense too.

I have been involved in many corporate responsibility drives over recent years and they are often cost-neutral if not cost-beneficial. My experience is by no means unique: there is a not-for-profit organization in the UK called WRAP. Its stated goals are to divert 8 million tonnes of waste materials from landfill, save 5 million tonnes of CO_2 equivalent emissions, and to generate £1.1 billion of economic benefits to business, local authorities and consumers. In relation to this, many of the UK's food manufacturers and retailers have signed up to a voluntary code on packaging reduction known as the Courtauld Commitment. You only need to look at some of their published case studies to see that an environmental agenda can make real commercial sense: Marks & Spencer recently introduced new packaging for its joints of beef that both reduced the amount of packaging by two-thirds and increased the freshness of the meat by up to four extra days. Britvic plc reduced the height and weight of its plastic bottles for its Robinson's soft drinks, reducing plastic and cardboard usage as well as increasing the number of bottles on a pallet, which eliminated 1,500 lorry loads each year. Proctor & Gamble has improved the manufacturing of Arial Excel Gel and has taken over 40 per cent water and energy out of the manufacturing process and a similar amount from its transport costs. Each of these case studies shows that economic and environmental common sense go hand-in-hand (WRAP, 2009).

Health, safety and environment

Long before corporate responsibility became the mantra, most organizations talked about health, safety and environment (HSE). While narrower in focus, many of its aspirations are similar, with organizations keen to fulfil ethical obligations to employees, the public and the natural world. Once again the implications of such policies will vary across industries, and while office-based environments might be wrestling with the ergonomics of desk configurations, heavy industries will be facing much more complex and challenging issues.

With significant issues come significant costs. Take a major construction or production site with a large number of employees and contractors, where simple health and safety training can costs thousands of days of downtime to both the site owner and its suppliers. Factors like this can create barriers to entry that prevent the participation of smaller suppliers. Equally, they can raise switching costs to prohibitive levels, as once a supplier's staff are trained no one has the appetite to go through the learning process again. This brings me nicely onto the last theme to cover under the theme of corporate responsibility.

Supplier diversity

Since the 1960s the United States has had legislation, particularly focused on public sector procurement, to promote the use of minority-owned vendors as suppliers. This type of positive discrimination is also pursued in other countries such as Canada and Australia, with a particular focus on aboriginal minorities. Increasingly the private sector is recognizing the value of supplier diversity to its businesses. The approach taken in Europe has tended to focus more on the creation of a level playing field, with European Union legislation insisting on open sourcing processes.

Every company can benefit from both concentrating the majority of its expenditure with its key suppliers and seeking niche, local or emerging suppliers for non-critical and low value spend. In this way companies can play a part in growing new businesses and supporting the regional economy.

In summary

In recent years the focus of the public on the behaviour of companies towards the environment in which they operate has put corporate responsibility firmly on the agenda of all companies. However, what each company needs to take responsibility for depends on the nature of the business it operates within. Corporate responsibility for any organization cannot stop at its doors. Instead, the corporate responsibility agenda should be pushed through supply chains into the tiers of suppliers that support it. Careful implementation of your corporate responsibility agenda can deliver both brand and economic enhancements. Truly, corporate responsibility doesn't have to cost the Earth.

16 Good procurement across the company

If procurement in your organization is in a mess, you need to put your arms around it. You need to wrest control and sort it out. But once it has been improved, once you know and are managing everything that you are spending across the organization, once you have the right contracts in place and the right people, processes and systems, then you might need to let it go. No, this isn't as barmy an idea as you might think. We have already established that procurement is too important to be left to the procurement department. What we need to do therefore is create a procurement-proficient organization and what this requires is controlled delegation.

I remember years ago attending a presentation by IBM to BP. It was a fantastic procurement story. As everyone knows, IBM had a very rocky time in the early 1990s and a significant part of its recovery had been facilitated by the transformation of the way it managed its supply chains, procurement and key suppliers. The statistics were awesome, the evidence was clear and the audience was mesmerized and very keen to do just what IBM had done. Until that is, someone in the audience asked how IBM managed maverick behaviour (when the business just does what it wants to, in disregard of existing contracts and policy). It turned out that IBM had a 'three strikes and you're out' rule: fail to do the right thing three times and you leave the company. It obviously worked for IBM: its non-compliance rate was less than 0.25 per cent (I was surprised it was that high!) But what BP realized in that moment was that it would never work for them. BP's whole culture was, at least at that time, based on the philosophy of 'let a thousand flowers bloom' – in other words, it was a very laissez-faire, empowering-the-individual culture. This was the most extreme clash of cultures that I ever witnessed, with both parties ultimately realizing that what worked for one would not work for both. What this story shows is the importance of understanding the corporate culture when establishing the best way to build procurement sustainability into an organization.

In this chapter we explore how corporate culture influences the way procurement will work in your organization over the long term and some of the models that you might use, complete with their pros and cons.

Corporate culture and procurement

The story I have just told shows two companies that are almost complete opposites in terms of culture; most other companies will sit somewhere in the middle. I spent much of my early career in Shell and it was exactly that – it had a strong laissez-faire attitude but was by no means as entrepreneurial in approach as BP. There was always a feeling that BP at the time was the speedboat to Shell's supertanker.

One way of thinking about this is to look at the company as though it were an individual. If you do this and look at the company through a Neuro-Linguistic Programming (NLP) lens you could consider whether its orientation is more 'options' or 'procedures'.

An options person is one who likes to consider all the options before coming to a conclusion and can often be accused of procrastinating or reinventing the wheel. He or she is most likely to create a new procedure for something and yet the least likely to follow it. A procedures person on the other hand is one who likes a clear process to follow. This makes him or her naturally inclined to comply with agreed procedures, with the danger that the procedure itself becomes more important than the outcome. As with all things in NLP there is no right or wrong answer and no better or worse orientation; instead it is useful to understand this characteristic in order to understand how best to communicate with and influence the person (Moulden and Hutchinson, 2006). This is just like a corporation: there is no right or wrong answer regarding a corporate culture – it just helps to understand it when you are trying to influence the way it will behave.

Therefore IBM, which had a procedure and measurement-oriented culture as well as a clear understanding of the value of good procurement, leant itself well to its 'three strikes and you're out' approach to procurement compliance. Whereas in BP, at the time with its entrepreneurial and options-oriented culture, procurement compliance for its own sake was anathema and had to be explored and proved over and over again.

Neither of these models is necessarily optimal for the long haul. I would definitely subscribe to the former model if you need to drive procurement improvement quickly and efficiently to maximize value to the organization. However, the danger is that it becomes too bureaucratic and self-serving, and compliance to the procedure becomes the purpose rather than the enabler. In such a situation, outcomes can deteriorate and fail to deliver true value to the organization. The latter model, while rather painful if one has to keep revalidating the appropriateness of the approach, does make sure that process remains an enabler of value rather than the end in itself. The optimal model and the one that delivers most to those organizations that sit between these two extremes (and let's face it most organizations will be in this middle ground) is one of subsidiarity and federalism.

According to the *Oxford English Dictionary,* subsidiarity is 'the principle that a central authority should perform only those tasks which cannot be performed at a more local level'. This means that activities and decisions should be performed by those people who rely on the outcomes or, in other words, performed as close to the coal face as possible. This works well in a procurement environment, where you don't want a central ordering department but want the end users to call off what they need when they need it. It also means that when there isn't an agreed contract in place, the end user should be equipped to make his or her own procurement decisions.

Federalism is defined as 'an agreement amongst parties that they will work together on things that are of mutual concern or interest'. In a procurement environment this would apply to company-wide contracts, management of common suppliers, processes and systems – everything where economies of scale and sharing can be beneficial to the constituent parts.

The dual features of subsidiarity and federalism mean that the organization can be flexible and agile yet benefit from the organization's scale and collective power in the marketplace. However, they also demand that the people involved in this model are appropriately equipped to make the right procurement decisions locally (whether to approach suppliers or utilize company-wide contracts). This is why we need the organization to be procurement proficient.

Procurement proficiency

A few years ago I worked in an organization of over 60,000 people. On a bad day, I sometimes thought that there were 60,000 people who believed they were buyers. In reality and on the good days, I acknowledged that less than 10 per cent of the people in the organization were empowered to sign procurement contracts – but this was still thousands of staff. In addition, at least 40 per cent of the total organization could log onto our procurement systems and call off against existing contracts, which ranged from significant business-critical supply to low-value items such as stationery, or travel arrangements like booking flights, rail journeys and hotels. The good thing about the procurement systems was that they empowered people to call off against existing commercial deals, thereby encouraging compliance to contracts and making maverick behaviour more difficult. However, it still leaves unanswered the question of need and whether they really needed the things they bought – which company hasn't had a stationery amnesty where people are encouraged to bring out of their desk drawers all the unused pens and pencils they have stockpiled over the months and years?

Anyway, back to the thousands in the organization who were authorized to sign new contracts. The challenge was that we needed to equip these colleagues to understand the implications of the demand they generated, the contracts they signed, the suppliers they selected and the goods and services they acquired. My team was less than a quarter of a per cent of the total organization, with the vast majority of procurement decision makers sitting elsewhere. Imagine the improvement in procurement practices that we could deliver to the company we all worked for if we could improve the procurement proficiency of the whole organization, starting with those with the authority to sign contracts. This is more than merely about what we buy and from whom. We need people to spend money wisely but also to make sure that the terms and conditions under which we buy are protecting the interests of our organization and encouraging our suppliers to deliver the things that we value.

Over the years I have seen some really terrible contracts that organizations have signed up to, for example, the tiny supplier suddenly granted exclusive rights to supply a particular service to a huge organization with unlimited liability and no rights to terminate, not even for breach. Or the contract that guarantees volume or income to the supplier for a service the organization no longer needs or wants. I don't think anyone ever signs these contacts maliciously, but sign them they do. In an ideal world, also known as a procurement proficient company, no one would be allowed to sign a contract until he or she had been given at least some rudimentary training in contract law and therefore understands the implications of the pages of small print.

There must also be an agreed hierarchy that means that all people across the organization use group-wide contracts and preferred suppliers wherever they exist. This in turn requires that the requisitioner's starting assumption is that his or her needs can be met by the goods and services that are already available in existing contracts. This would help ensure that the requisitioner only thinks about looking for alternative specifications or sources of supply when all other avenues are exhausted. Sometimes it feels like the opposite is true. You need only look at the number of active suppliers in your purchase order and accounts payable systems to realize that variety and not consistency is the norm.

Many organizations have thousands of suppliers – yet probably fewer than a hundred of them are significant in terms of expenditure or important in respect of delivered value. This can be doubly frustrating when you think of the effort you have put in to establishing commercially attractive contracts for fit-for-purpose, good quality goods and services from reputable, financially sound suppliers – only to see the spend going elsewhere. It can also be commercially catastrophic because your preferred vendors will have offered their cost, service level and quality commitments based on an expected volume of business. Maverick behaviour means that this volume can be compromised, which in turn will damage relationships with key suppliers and mean that when re-tendered the suppliers are less interested in the work.

Whenever I embark on a procurement transformation programme I make sure that I get three things agreed by the board. The first is a mandate from them (it is not a panacea but it does help), the second is a budget that will achieve the goals of the transformation, and the third is a budget that will enable a step-change in people skills, processes and systems that will ensure sustainability of the benefits and new ways of working. The outcome of under-funded and under-supported programmes is usually a hockey stick-shaped cost profile – where the value is delivered in the short term but all the costs creep back up as soon as the programme is finished and the senior attention moves onto the next priority. I remember years ago talking to a senior exec in an organization who said that he thought he could take 7 per cent off his third-party budgets just by telling his direct reports that he was scrutinizing those costs lines. I am sure that he was right – but as soon as his attention waivered, those costs would be back in a nano-second plus extra in the form of a bow wave to compensate for the period of artificially suppressed demand and its related spend.

In summary

Driving cost out isn't difficult; keeping it out is the real challenge and for that the improvement programme needs a different focus. A key component of any sustainable transformation programme therefore has to include a procurement proficiency drive. A good procurement proficiency programme will effectively teach people to fish rather than throw them one.

17 Becoming important to key suppliers

Get your lipstick on

Do you remember the power dressing of the 1980s? Its proponents used to say that the power symbols for men were ties and belts, and for women they were earrings and lipstick. I suppose that is probably why I like to make sure that I have my lipstick on when going into tough meetings.

However, that isn't really what I mean by getting your lipstick on in this chapter; instead it is all about creating relationships with and making yourself attractive to your important suppliers. I used to use the words, 'Get your lipstick on' pretty regularly until the furore in September 2008 during the US Presidential race when the then Senator Obama said in a speech, 'You know, you can put lipstick on a pig, but it's still a pig,' and then continued, 'You can wrap an old fish in a piece of paper called "change." It's still gonna stink after eight years' (Earle, 2008).

Since all the fuss, I now use the phrase more circumspectly, but it probably makes the message more meaningful than ever. A lot of people pay lip-service (with or without the lipstick) to their supplier relationships and don't actually mean very much by it. This is rather crazy when key suppliers are integral to the success of both your value propositions and your organization.

In this chapter we are going to explore how you can make your organization attractive to your suppliers throughout your relationship with them and how you can ensure that both you and your suppliers do everything possible to make these relationships mutually beneficial. Interestingly, smaller companies are often better at creating sustainable relationships with their suppliers than larger ones are. Large companies sometimes take a step backward rather than forward when dealing with their suppliers – keeping the relationships at arm's length. The smaller, more entrepreneurial companies, however, will constantly ask their suppliers questions such as 'What can you do for me?'; 'What can we do together?' and, 'What have I got to trade?'

Becoming important

In an earlier chapter we explored what suppliers want from their customers and recognized that while revenue is important, many other factors such as profit, shared strategic ambition, cultural fit, brand recognition and the A-list status of their customers all played a part. We are now going to explore some of the ways in which you, as a customer, can tap into these other aspects and ensure that you are as attractive as possible to the suppliers you want to do business with.

A lot of suppliers go to the trouble of commissioning independent researchers to find out what their customers think of them. I think this is great. Unfortunately, not many customers commission surveys to understand what their suppliers think of them. However, there are some pan-industry surveys, such as the Annual North American Automotive OEM – Tier 1 Supplier Working Relations Study conducted by Planning Perspectives Inc, which is now in its ninth year. This survey investigates tier one supplier relationships with North American domestic original equipment manufacturers (OEM) of GM, Ford and Chrysler and the foreign domestic OEM of Toyota, Honda and Nissan. Interestingly, the survey recognizes clear value for the OEM of being preferred customers of their tier one suppliers in terms of receiving lower costs, higher quality and innovation than unfavoured rivals (PPI, 2009).

Tangible value can be generated through good relationships because, while some companies are naturally very good at working with their suppliers, others are not. There are lots of reasons for this and we are going to explore some now.

Good relationships

In the beginning

I think that by now you probably know exactly what I am going to say about this. The start of any good relationship with your supplier must be that both of you clearly understand what need you are trying to satisfy. This has to happen right from the beginning of the tender process. You articulate what you need and the suppliers tell you how they could satisfy it. You evaluate each of the suppliers' solutions against your requirements and pick the one that seems most appropriate. A needs statement will have many facets and be supported by different criteria such as compatibility of your corporate responsibility agendas, business strategies and culture. The process will hopefully result in your selecting supplier(s) that you feel will meet your requirements over both the short and longer term, as well as understanding and complementing your strategic priorities. So far, so good.

At this point don't be fooled by camaraderie and good will. What you have been through is a courtship – both organizations have seen the best of each other. You will have obviously done your due diligence: the reference and site visits, tested the proposed solution, and met the key people who will be supporting you post-contract award. All of which is good stuff. However, what you now need is the contract, that document that will define your relationship with your supplier, specify the reward for and safeguard the delivery of the things that you value, and will ultimately provide certain protections to both parties if things don't go as planned.

Don't leave it to the lawyers

The contract is something that you and the supplier are going to have to live with when the lawyers have gone home. To some extent it is the cornerstone of your relationship and therefore it is very important that both you and your supplier are absolutely content with and fully understand it. It is a constant surprise to me that the client and supplier organizations often leave this in the hands of others to draft and finalize. It is almost treated like a prenuptial agreement – in the eyes of the bride and groom a rather grubby must-have, which if invoked will have demonstrated that the marriage shouldn't have happened in the first place.

This is not what a supply contract is all about. It is actually defining your relationship – what good or service the supplier is going to deliver to you, when and for what reward, and what you are going to deliver to your supplier, when and to what end. Imagine the conversations that have gone on during the courtship, starting with the supplier saying, 'Well, if you need the first prototype by 1 November, we need to have your final specifications by 3 March at the latest' and the client's response: 'No problem. We will have the specs by the end of February at the latest', and both parties nodding and smiling and both knowing that the deadlines are tight and there is no room for error.

I spent two days a week for almost two years of my life negotiating a settlement on a contract that had gone wrong. It had gone wrong because, despite being the size of *War and Peace*, the contract was nowhere near the quality of Tolstoy's masterpiece and, to be quite honest, most of its contents were subject to interpretation. There was a whole section of the document that showed the technical specification that the supplier had submitted to meet its client's needs – which would have been great but actually (by mutual consent) that wasn't what it started to deliver. Equally, there were lots of references to the physical solution and very few to what the client needed the solution to deliver. And yet, because there were very few people still around who had been involved in the tender, selection and contracting process, it was quite literally the only document that both parties had to go on. In fact one of the few people still around was one of the third-party lawyers who had been involved in drafting the contract, which made the whole process even more expensive and convoluted to resolve.

Another issue we had to grapple with in this particular instance was that there was really nowhere else to go. The switching costs and time needed to get another solution with a new vendor were both eye-watering and totally unfeasible. We had to reach a mutually acceptable solution and remove the commercial and contractual barriers – that was what they had become, with both the supplier and client loathe to have honest conversations about where they were and what they needed to do in case this became evidence if the whole thing went to court. If we could not find such a solution, we were just going to stay in the nightmare where both organizations were losing money and delivering sub-standard service to their customers.

So despite how good you feel about each other in the early days of the relationship, make sure that your scope of work is robust, articulates clearly both your responsibilities and those of your supplier, specifies the required outputs and service levels and a payment structure that rewards their attainment; and ultimately that the terms and conditions include a framework for dispute resolution and deliver all the protections that both parties need. Most of all, make sure that you have an exit strategy and fall-back plan, and that if these are going to be impossible to make work then ensure that everyone knows it from the get-go.

It might be painful and time-consuming to get a contract that makes sense and is acceptable to both parties; it might be difficult once everything is laid out in the contract to get anyone in either company to sign up to it – but better that than to sail blithely into a relationship that is destined to fail. A good contract is worth its weight in gold and, ironically, by being good, shouldn't necessarily weigh much.

Getting what it says on the tin

All of the work that you have put into your requirements specification, supplier selection process and contract are building nicely to the point where you have the right supplier capable of and contracted to deliver just what your organization and its customers need. So all we need to do now is make sure that you and your supplier deliver on your promises.

Ideally the people who are now responsible for delivery have been involved since this project was just a twinkle in somebody's eye. Sometimes that just isn't possible, in which case an in-depth handover will have been planned. Unfortunately, at other times, what needs to happen post-contract hasn't even been thought of and the slick-suited sales team are replaced by the chumps on the hook for delivery, and the client organization just breathes a sigh of relief, ticks this off its to-do list and puts the contract in the bottom drawer with a sense that the job has been done.

In reality the job hasn't even started and the lack of focus on delivery has just made the chances of success take a nose-dive. The supplier needs a client services manager who understands your operational requirements in this post-contract period and is on the hook for making sure that it delivers on its promises, and someone in your organization to work hand-in-glove with to make sure that the objectives of the contract will be secured.

Securing what you need

The amount of effort and the criteria for success in this relationship will depend on how important the good or service you are receiving is to your business, and this takes us nicely back to one of my favourite two-by-two models that I introduced in Chapter 11. In Figure 17.1 I have overlaid the model from Figure 11.2 with additional information that relates to the type of relationship with your suppliers that is most appropriate in light of their importance to your business. Moving from left to right and up the matrix, these are deliver, align and collaborate.

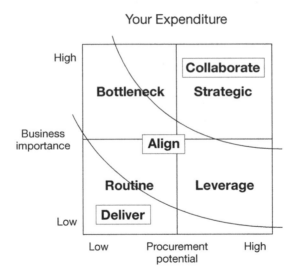

Figure 17.1 Supplier relationship strategies

Deliver

The management effort required for suppliers whose goods and services fall into the bottom left segment on the diagram will be basic and should be focused on receiving the scope of work as specified in the contract – basically you just want 'what is says on the tin'. The relationship is likely to be rather transactional. You will have a supplier scorecard but it will focus on the more mundane aspects such as delivery on their side and payment on yours, as well as operational matters associated with such things as quality, timeliness, corporate responsibility and health and safety.

Align

Relationships that fall under the broad, middle swathe of the diagram are, for a variety of different reasons, likely to be complex and require significant focus. Some might be important because you spend a fortune with the supplier, and others because you spend little but what it delivers is absolutely critical to you. The buyer/supplier dynamic is also likely to range from those that are evenly balanced to others where the supplier seems to be holding all the cards (for example, it might be a monopoly provider to you).

However, from a relationship point of view, you not only need 'what it says on the tin', you will also want to ensure that there is some transparency and alignment between your organizations. For example, you will want to know each other's business strategies to ensure that, where appropriate, they are aligned for mutual benefit. Equally, you will be keen to safeguard continuity of supply and therefore are likely to study the supplier's business performance and other key indicators.

While relationships that fall under 'deliver' are likely to be managed at operational levels in both organizations, those that fall under 'align' are likely to have more senior and strategic oversight. In addition to the hygiene factors mentioned above, the supplier scorecard is likely to cover dimensions such as continuous improvement and systems alignment, all of which recognize that the supplier's activities on your behalf are important to your business.

Collaborate

The final dimension sweeps across the upper part of the chart, picking up most of the goods and services that have been classified as 'strategic' and a lot of those in 'bottleneck'. These are the most critical of the goods and services that you receive from suppliers and are inextricably linked to your overall success. Therefore, when you manage the relationship you need to measure not only the hygiene and added-value features as described under 'deliver' and 'align', but also promote a more collaborative culture between the organizations. Continuous improvement as described earlier is still very focused upon the supplier and the good or service it delivers to you.

Collaboration starts to move towards broader alliances where you might consider joint ventures and research and development projects. At its extremes, this is the sort of territory that companies like Microsoft and Intel inhabit together, where the sum of the parts is greater than the whole and where the pinnacle of the relationships will ultimately reside in the boardrooms of both organizations. Needless to say, there will not be many of these types of relationships and some will be a little more mundane; nevertheless, the underlying characteristics and objectives will remain the same.

Wherever the relationship plots on this chart, the ambition should always be to ensure that the relationship is fit-for-purpose and delivers appropriately for both the client and supplier organizations. Key to this will be honesty, respect and mutual value.

Complexity

Of course it's never that simple. For example, you are likely to have many different relationships with some suppliers, particularly the large ones. These relationships vary in complexity and importance and could therefore be plotted all over the grid. Similarly, you are likely to have multi-faceted relationships with some companies where each of you is both a buyer and a supplier to the other. Finally and probably most difficult will be the relationships that are critical to you but invisible – for example a critical sub-component manufacturer that sits in either tier two or three of your supply chain and with which therefore you do not have a direct relationship.

There are various things that you can do to manage all of this complexity – it just needs a bit more attention. Where you have multiple relationships with the same supplier you need to manage the contracts separately by following the strategies I have outlined above. At the same time you need to look holistically at the supplier and manage the relationship with it as a single entity. In this way you are probably going to have an executive-sponsor for the supplier overall and various supplier managers dotted around the organization, all to ensure that the contracts deliver, on the one hand, and that you are strategically aligned on the other. One thing that I have found works very well for the most complex of these is setting up an internal executive committee that leverages the full extent of the relationship and makes sure that bad and good service are visible and are being managed holistically. In addition to the internal committee there is a supplier executive committee where the senior people from both organizations come together to provide strategic focus and scrutiny. Being seen to have an understanding of all aspects of a supplier's business with you helps to ensure that all of its components are delivering value to your company.

Where both organizations are suppliers and buyers to each other this can get a little tricky and sometimes requires the creation of Chinese Walls between the different relationships. Key to success in all such cases is to assess each business opportunity separately and ensure that each stands or falls on its own merits. Obviously, where all things are equal, it makes sense to let the breadth of the relationship be the deciding vote, but misery awaits all parties if too much favour is shown because of it.

Probably the most difficult relationships to manage are those that are not visible to the client. A few years ago I worked to solve a problem where a sub-contractor of a systems integrator was in financial difficulty. Had the company failed, a large part of the integrator's service to my customer would have ceased and yet, in theory, we had no relationship with that subcontractor and were reliant on influencing and auditing the integrator's contingency arrangements. What this taught me was how important it is, when reviewing supply continuity risks, to ensure that you include critical subcontractors in the process. A slightly longer-term problem that can arise in these supplier tiers is that they are very far from the customer value proposition and you need to work especially hard to keep them connected to it, especially if you expect innovation and improvement to come from that level in the supply hierarchy.

Supplier management

To some extent I think that supplier and contract management is the final frontier of great procurement because it is something that I am not yet convinced we do very well in most organizations. Certainly until a few years ago most procurement departments happily threw the signed contract over the wall to the business that was destined to receive the goods and services and just moved on to the next sourcing assignment. What most of us failed to realize was that nothing of value is delivered to the organization until the contract is being used. An ignored contract isn't worth the paper it is written on and an unknown contract is worth even less. A contract is *ignored* when the business carries on buying whatever it wants from its favourite supplier; this maverick behaviour can be very costly to the organization. A contract is *unknown* when the business doesn't understand the full provisions of the supply agreement (and let's face it some are very complicated), and ends up paying again for something that is already included in the terms, or doesn't understand or enforce the agreed levels of service.

Despite these pitfalls, it is also true that supplier and contract management is pretty expensive to do well. Even though the rewards are significant and tangible, many executives believe that 'costs are certain and value delivery is just wishful thinking'. This attitude alone can scupper your chances of proving them wrong if it means that you cannot secure the correct level of investment. A reasonable rule of thumb for the cost of managing a complex contract for critical, usually outsourced, services is that it will cost between 2 and 4 per cent of its annual value. This would mean that a contract with an annual value of £10 million will cost between £200,000 and £400,000 to manage.

For such complex contracts the supplier management team is often referred to as the 'retained layer'. A retained layer will comprise a variety of skills including technical understanding of the services being received. This retained layer is a key way in which the business continues to understand the services being received and remains an intelligent buyer over time.

There are several dangers that companies face when they outsource an activity, the two extremes of which are 'shadows' and 'voids'. Sometimes a company outsources the activity but keeps in-house some of the people who used to manage the activity. This is a good idea provided that the people are re-skilled to become the retained layer, but is a very bad idea if they are just left to shadow the outsourced service providers. What I have seen happen in such a situation is that the shadow is now distant from the sharp end of the service, and his or her skills become outdated, but he or she continues to second-guess and instruct the service provider on the technicalities of the solution instead of specifying and vetting delivery against the functional requirements. This can cause frustration on both sides and ultimately may mean that the solutions implemented are suboptimal.

A void is unfortunately just that – the service is outsourced and all the experts either move to the supplier or are lost. In such situations the void means that the client neither has the expertise to specify and vet delivery against the functional specification nor the capability in-house to define what 'good' looks like. This is a dangerous situation for the client to be in, both during the period of the contract and especially when the contract is up for re-tender.

An outsourcing contract between Xerox and EDS in the 1990s stands as one of the notable cases of how it can go wrong. In 1994, Xerox handed over the responsibility for running its IT systems to EDS, including critical applications like billing and sales-commission systems. Xerox's objective was not to save costs but to 'enable IT to focus on new systems and strategies'. Along with the systems, their IT talent transferred over to EDS and Xerox no longer had the capability to make any changes to its legacy systems. As the service provision progressed, EDS discovered it had little scope to make a profit other than by standardizing technology and by introducing greater uniformity of systems, so to manage its own costs better it implemented a rigid fixed-cost model for change requests. Xerox decided that it wasn't getting the service for which it had contracted and refused to pay the bills it received, ultimately causing EDS to write off US$200 million in 1998 and then sue Xerox for non-payment of invoices. When conditions in its markets changed later that year, Xerox had to reorganize its sales and marketing operations. The ongoing dispute between the two companies impacted the implementation of the required changes to the systems, leaving Xerox unable to bill its customers and, in reaction to this, its share price fell dramatically (Strassmann, 2000).

Interestingly, the lawsuit was resolved by expanding the relationship between the two companies. In September 2001, EDS signed a five-year, US$50 million contract with Xerox to include Xerox products and services as part of EDS's Navy intranet contract. The following December, Xerox signed a five-year, US$1.5 billion extension to the outsourcing contract it had signed in 1994 (Greenemeier, 2001). Over recent years, Xerox and EDS have built strong alliances for delivering services to corporate customers.

The silver bullet

I suppose the short answer if you are looking for a silver bullet to make sure that your suppliers live up to their promises is that you also live up to yours. Sometimes buying organizations can get quite irrational about relationships with their suppliers and think it is a one-way street with the supplier on the hook for everything. A good relationship is grounded in a full understanding of the job at hand, clear roles and responsibilities assigned to each party, value for both parties, and open channels of communication at the right level in the companies' hierarchies to keep things on the right track.

In summary

The signing of a contract is the beginning of a relationship between your organization and your supplier. The nature of that relationship depends on its importance to you. The types of relationships you may enter into can range from simple transactional delivery management to complex multifaceted relationships that need to be managed holistically. However, with all contracts, the reality is that the value is not delivered until the contract is used, and it is when the contract is used that issues can occur. It is by active management of the relationship that problems get resolved and the value you signed up for gets delivered.

In the next couple of chapters I am going to start to explore the concept of continuous improvement and re-engineering but to be quite honest, without getting the relationships on an even keel first, this is just a pipedream.

18 Continuous improvement

Don't be fooled by mediocrity

You have a good relationship with your supplier that is underpinned by a great contract that delivers what you need, encourages the behaviours you value and contains a clause to encourage continuous improvement and share the proceeds. All the boxes are ticked and you are feeling pretty smug.

While I don't want to rain on your parade, because congratulations are definitely in order, I do want to introduce a note of caution here. The existence of a clause in your contract about continuous improvement and gainshare doesn't automatically mean that improvements will be continuously delivered or even delivered at all. Continuous improvement is difficult to achieve at best and under some circumstances can actually be counterproductive.

There has been a lot written about the automotive industry and its relationship with its suppliers. On the one hand you have companies that are held up as exemplars, such as the large Japanese manufacturers that have worked collaboratively with their suppliers for decades. On the other hand you have the US giants such as GM and Ford that have a history of more adversarial relationships with their suppliers (Hannon, 2007).

The cautionary tale that I want to share involved a US automotive manufacturer that had been running a programme of continuous improvement with its key suppliers, which successfully delivered a year-on-year cost reduction. This made and kept the procurement department, the automotive company and its suppliers happy. Then came the dot com era. One of the weirdest phenomena that happened during all the e-hype was the emergence everywhere of industry-specific vertical eVentures. One of the first out of the stocks was Covisint, which was the automotive vertical marketplace. The concept behind the vertical marketplace was that the member automotive manufacturers could collaborate for mutual benefit. Whatever lofty ambitions this pan-industry body had, they were stymied pretty quickly when the US regulators decided that any attempts to leverage the scale of its member companies would be anti-competitive. Soon after this ruling, Covisint became little more than an eMarketplace with tools such as eProcurement and eAuctions available to its members.

To secure value from the vast amounts of money they had sunk into the venture, several automotive manufacturers started to use the eAuction product set and within a couple of years, several billion dollars worth of business had been sourced using it. For those who are not familiar with the concept of eAuctions, it is basically an online interactive tool that allows suppliers to bid in real time for a client's business. eAuctions can be very sophisticated and involve a variety of financial and non-financial selection criteria. Some people hate them and others love them; I for one think they have their place in a sourcing process but that they should never be used as the sole decision support tool.

Anyway, back to my story. Everyone was happy with the continuous improvements that were being made until someone decided to auction tyres, which had been one of the categories that had been subject to continuous improvement. After years of achieving gradual reductions, suddenly, in an event that probably took less than an hour to complete, the cost of tyres to the automotive manufacturer went down over 15 per cent. Undoubtedly there were many reasons for this, including the fact that the event had provided the first occasion in several years for companies to compete for the business, and the supply market responded aggressively to this opportunity. However, it is hard not to think that there must have been complacency creeping into the cosy world of continuous improvement with both buyers and suppliers going through the motions and playing the game. It is easy to imagine a situation whereby a manufacturing breakthrough or the like had significantly reduced tyre production costs but that the benefits were being drip-fed, little by little, each year to the client. It probably goes without saying that in a margin-challenged automotive industry this outcome caused huge ructions and heralded the return of the less collaborative best-of-three quotes approach to procurement.

In this example, continuous improvement seems to have become a synonym for incrementalism and mediocrity and is one of the reasons I say that continuous improvement is a particular challenge. In this chapter, we are going to explore the true benefits of this value driver (because there are many) as well as investigating some of the associated myths and pitfalls, and with some strategies to avoid them.

Getting the organization on side

I still remember the first time that I had to take a contract that contained a continuous improvement clause to a board meeting to get sign-off. The contract itself was quite complicated and the cost to the company was tens of millions of pounds over its five-year duration. We had worked out to the nth degree what this meant to the supplier in terms of both revenue and profit margin. Everything was going fine, and then we came to the gainshare clause. Basically the idea was that for anything more than a £100,000 reduction in our annual costs that the supplier helped us to deliver we were going to give the supplier 20 per cent of the amount saved. Table 18.1 illustrates the principle and assumes that the cost reduction initiative delivered £250,000.

Table 18.1   Gainshare example

Buying organization	£k	Supplier	£k	profit %
Forecast cost pa	5,000	Revenue	5,000	
		Margin	250	5
Cost reduction eg	-200	Gainshare	50	
Forecast cost pa	4,800	Margin	240	
Revised costs pa	4,800	Margin	290	6

What the model shows is the cost to the buying organization reducing by £200,000 (4 per cent) and the supplier receiving £50,000 as a bonus. The amount the supplier received increased the profitability of the contract for them by 16 per cent (from £250,000 to £290,000). To my mind this seems like a real win-win for both the client whose expenditure was reduced by £200,000 and the supplier whose profitability increased by £40,000. I don't know if it was the percentages that got the board spooked (4 per cent cost reduction versus 16 per cent margin improvement) but whatever it was, it took me ages to persuade them that it was to their benefit and get the deal approved.

I think this was the first time I encountered the attitude that all the benefit must belong to the buying organization and that there was absolutely no need to provide additional incentive for the supplier because its reward would be winning and potentially keeping the work. What this example also illustrates is that amounts that seem quite trivial can have a huge impact on the supplier's profitability and as such provide a very strong incentive to improve.

The same again but on steroids

Another example of this on a much larger scale is Chrysler's Supplier Cost Reduction Effort (SCORE) programme that was launched in the late 1980s and ran very successfully until the company was bought by Daimler over a decade later (see wwww.allpar.com, accessed February 2010). Over this period Chrysler, more than any other US automotive manufacturer, embraced the ethos of genuine collaboration and gainshare with its suppliers. It did this for both new and existing products and as such reaped significant rewards. I want to share this example with you despite its age because Chrysler managed to do something that neither GM nor Ford has ever managed to do. As illustrated in the previous example, continuous improvement and gainshare require a huge mindset shift in any organization. To move a US automotive manufacturer away from the best-of-three quotes approach and a very old school, adversarial relationship between buyer and sellers was an incredible achievement. So how was it done?

One of the first things it did was benchmark itself against Honda in the mid-1980s. This revealed that Honda's supplier selection criteria included factors such as the relationship between the buyer and seller, the seller's quality record and its historic ability to meet cost targets. None of this is rocket science to good procurement – but it was a revelation to Chrysler whose first, second and third selection criteria had all been price.

Received wisdom at the time was that Japanese approaches wouldn't work in the United States. Luckily for Chrysler it had just bought AMC (at the time the fourth largest car maker in the United States), which had been dabbling with Japanese techniques and was enjoying significant success in decreasing development cycle time and getting new products to market (something that Chrysler desperately wanted to do better). AMC's visible success dealt a blow to those sceptics who challenged the transferability of Japanese practices into US companies.

Equally important was the fact that the acquisition of AMC had created Chrysler's equivalent of a burning platform: the company was saddled with huge debt and therefore needed to cut its costs. Finally, there were enough of the very senior leaders of the company, including Thomas Stallkamp, the then Procurement Director who ultimately went on to become CEO, in favour of the transformation. This was important, especially in the early days when many in the middle layers of the organization did not want to accept or implement supplier-suggested improvements to either the components they made or the processes to which they contributed.

The results of the SCORE programme speak for themselves in respect of new product introduction and collaborative design. By 1996 SCORE initiatives represented a cost reduction to Chrysler of over US$1 billion in that year alone. This probably brings me to the final, final reason that SCORE succeeded in Chrysler – it had a robust and clearly articulated way of measuring benefits, and savings only counted when cost was visibly removed from the supply chain and not just reallocated elsewhere (Braun *et al*, accessed February 2010).

Unfortunately, the footnote to this story is not so positive and is a salutary tale of the importance of executive commitment to such a programme. When Daimler bought Chrysler, this approach to supplier management was gradually unwound and more traditional procurement practices resumed. It is sad to note that Chrysler is now the worst OEM as analysed in the Annual North American Automotive OEM – Tier One Supplier Working Relationship Study (PPI, 2009).

Still on steroids, but this time even more complex

As mentioned in the example above, one of the key phases in which buyer-supplier collaboration can deliver significant value is product development. However, one of the biggest challenges to true collaboration during the development of a product or solution can be when the relationship isn't a linear one between a buyer and a single supplier. When you look at any supply chain you can see that there are potentially many tier one suppliers that will have a role to play in making your product or solution a success, and of course this becomes even more complex when you start to factor in the various tiers of other suppliers that are supporting your main suppliers.

One of the biggest challenges that must be overcome in the creation of a truly collaborative environment is the fact that only one of the parties holds the purse strings. This might not be too much of a challenge where that party is fulfilling only the role of the client in the programme; it becomes much more complicated when the client is also part of the consortium determining the solution. The challenge is to make sure that the client doesn't hold inappropriate sway over the decision-making process because if it does, the whole spirit of collaboration and excellence can be undermined.

This happened a lot in the oil and gas industry, with notionally collaborative programmes kicking off only to founder because the client ultimately held more of the power and made more of the decisions. One of the operators overcame this with a simple but effective organizational twist. Effectively it split its roles into two – one as the budget holder and ultimate client for the programme and the other as a supplier helping to deliver the most appropriate solution. In its role as supplier the operator joined other key suppliers in a Camelot-like round table where all suppliers had equal say on design decisions and equal call on the gainshare pot generated through the improvements that they delivered. In its other role as operator it continued to play its traditional role as client to the round table of suppliers. This worked incredibly well and brought many innovative solutions into production in the North Sea – usually under budget and ahead of schedule.

The magic ingredients for continuous improvement

I hope, based on these examples, you will agree with me that most organizations can benefit from the introduction of a programme of continuous improvement and gainshare. However, there are many pitfalls, not the least of which can be the buying organization's resistance to changing the way that it treats its suppliers.

The success factors include bedrock pricing – making sure that the original contract already reflects the lowest cost (use all the usual tools such as should-cost modelling, competitive tendering and negotiation). If the starting point is too high, all you will succeed in doing is paying the supplier for the privilege of taking five years to get to the pricing that you should have been enjoying from day one. One of the most important reasons for getting to bedrock pricing therefore is that the whole initiative can be undermined if the buying organization starts to feel that it is being tricked into sharing benefits with the supplier that should have been enjoyed by it alone.

This brings me nicely on to the second of the success factors, which is measurement. It is important that there is a robust and agreed mechanism for the way in which costs are baselined and tested, and against which savings are identified, quantified and shared amongst the participating organizations.

I am going to lump together gainshare and culture because getting the principles of gainshare clearly understood and visibly supported by the most senior levels in your organization will help to shift the culture of the organization towards acceptance. In this way you will tackle head-on any issues associated with the way in which suppliers are viewed in your organization. If you are really struggling to get the right levels of collaboration across your organization, don't be afraid to take a leaf out of the oil operator's book and create a programme structure that is capable of overcoming those problems.

Finally, don't forget the value of humility and make sure that you are humble enough to find out what others are doing and be prepared, where appropriate, to copy them. Don't forget imitation is the greatest form of flattery.

19 Reducing total cost

Shrinking the pie

This may seem a rather odd title for this section, but actually it is a very accurate label for the contents. If you assume that the 'pie' is the total cost of the good or service that you are acquiring for either your organization or your customers, then 'shrinking it' is all about reducing that total cost. There is a strong relationship between the continuous improvement that we covered in the last chapter and this, because shrinking the pie is all about re-engineering activities, which also happens to be one of the best ways of delivering continuous improvement. The main difference is that continuous improvement starts once the contract has been signed, while shrinking the pie can happen at any point in the procurement process.

As we have already discovered, there are many ways of reducing the costs of the good or service to the acquiring organization and the fastest of these is to cut the prices you are willing to pay for it. Initially this is likely to pay dividends, particularly if you haven't been managing the acquisition process very effectively and therefore the supplier is complacent and its margins are chubby. Similarly, if you manage to create order out of chaos and commit volume to a supplier or standardize the things you buy from it, you can expect to secure a unit price reduction. These are the sorts of opportunities that help you get to the 'bedrock' that we talked about in the last chapter, and as such these sorts of initiatives are going to get you to the point where you are comfortable that the margin the supplier is making on your business is appropriate. I would always recommend this as a good first step – using the simple levers initially to cut away the excess.

Obviously you could continue to use these levers, but at some point their impact will reduce and, if you end up squeezing too hard, will start to backfire. Either cost will creep in somewhere (after all, the supplier does have to make a profit) or the quality of what you are buying and the services associated with it will erode and therefore the value of what you are buying will diminish. The challenge therefore is, once you have done the easy and obvious stuff, what to do next.

You might have noticed that in the above paragraphs I have used a word that I almost never do, which is 'price'. I hardly ever use it because good and sustainable procurement improvement isn't about price but about optimizing total cost and securing value. This is where the concept of shrinking the pie comes in. What a great outcome it would be if you managed to reduce the total cost of the good or service you are buying and yet enable the supplier to make a reasonable, even an increased, margin on this reduced spend. If you think back to one of the examples I went through in the last chapter, where the costs went down by £200,000 to the client and at the same time profits increased £40,000 to the supplier – this is exactly what we did. We shrank the pie through transformation of our own and the supplier's costs.

In this chapter we are going to explore the concept of shrinking the pie in much more detail, starting with total cost.

Total cost of ownership

This term refers to the total cost to your organization of using a good or a service to support your customer value proposition or for some other purpose. Everything from the humble pencil to an aeroplane has a total cost of ownership. Let's start with the pencil and work our way up.

Figure 19.1 illustrates the client's supply chain for the pencil (starting with the identification of its need and ending with its disposal) as well as the supply chain of the stationery provider (starting with product research and finishing with after-sales service). You will see that the intersection of these two supply chains is the price that the client is willing to pay. The *total cost* to the client organization will be the activities in its supply chain, including the price paid to the supplier.

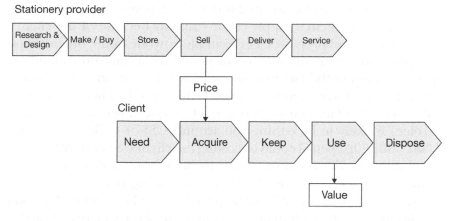

Figure 19.1 The client's supply chain for a pencil

By the way, this example illustrates nicely why 'price' is a logical place to start when trying to optimize your costs as it is the obvious intersection between the two supply chains. It is also third-party expenditure and as such is very visible to your organization in a way that internal costs associated with a particular supply chain are not. Remember that the executive's cry of, 'We spend how much?' was all about the expenditure through accounts payable. It is a much more sophisticated executive who cries, 'It costs how much?' in respect of a supply chain where the costs are going to be a combination of internal and external expenditure. It explains why pencils are such a great example because I can guarantee that the invoiced amount on pencils is going to be only a fraction of their total cost of ownership to the client. To illustrate this let's look in a little more detail at the cost and value drivers in the client's supply chain.

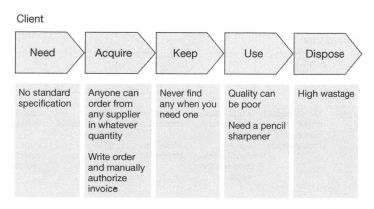

Figure 19.2 Cost and value drivers in client supply for pencils

What you can see in Figure 19.2 is that there is significant cost being driven into the client's supply chain – mainly because of the client's own practices and processes. For example, anyone in the organization can place an order for any type of pencil from any supplier in any quantity (despite the fact that presumably it has an agreed stationery list with its preferred vendor). If you factor into the client's total cost calculation the fact that each order set (request, order, receipt and invoice) is likely to be costing you around US$70 (GBP £50) then a US$1 (GBP 50p) pencil could be costing the client US$71 (GBP £50.50) to acquire. As there doesn't seem to be any network of stationery cupboards, each person is potentially stockpiling pencils. If the user doesn't have a sharpener then the pencil's useful life will end as soon as it is blunt (ok, that might be a stretch). One of the sobering thoughts when you look at a supply chain like this is that value is only added to the organization at the point of use. If the pencil is languishing in a drawer, unused and unloved, it is just a cost. Only when the pencil is being used to write, draw or whatever other purpose it was bought for, is it adding any value.

From this simple example it is fairly obvious that whatever 'price' the client is paying for its pencils, the true total cost of ownership is much higher and it is also obvious that there are a lot of things that the client could do to re-engineer its supply chain and remove cost. It could do this in isolation from its supplier but, as we saw with consequential supply chains in earlier chapters, point improvements rather than holistic change can inadvertently drive cost into related supply chain – in this case the supplier's. So, before we decide what improvements to make, let's look at the stationery provider's own supply chain, in Figure 19.3, and analyse the impact the client's supply chain is having on it.

Stationery provider

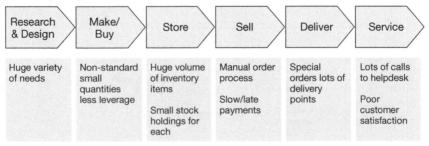

Figure 19.3 Cost and value drivers of a stationery provider's supply chain

The fact that the client is requesting lots of non-standard items in small quantities (sometimes with competing suppliers) is inhibiting the stationery provider's ability to predict and leverage volume with its own suppliers. It is also being forced to keep a broad range of inventory lines just in case the client wants to order them, which in turn means that its stock holdings of particular items can be quite low (as it needs to manage its inventory costs), so there is an increased risk of stock-outs (which might, in turn, mean that the client is placing 'special orders' that are more expensive to both client and supplier). The order process is manual and clunky and is leading to instances of late payment, which is impacting the supplier's cash flow. Finally, because the process is so fragmented and opaque there are a huge number of calls to the helpdesk. Overall, the client's custom is costing its preferred stationery provider a small fortune to satisfy and, of course, ultimately some or all of this will be reflected in the price the customer pays.

This is why total cost is important and why re-engineering of your supply chain and its interactions with those of your suppliers can help to 'shrink the pie' and deliver radical and sustainable cost reduction. And if you can collaborate with your supplier to re-engineer your processes such that both your costs and those of your supplier reduce, would you really care if its profit margin went up? This is the essence of shrinking the pie.

Obviously in this example you have already selected your supplier and therefore it is potentially easier to undertake this analysis and deliver the value. However, one of the challenges you will face is the appetite and ability of the supplier to support your re-engineering ambition. Just staying with our pencils for a moment, if all the other customers of the stationery provider are as badly organized as the client we examined, then changing the process for only you might actually drive cost into the stationery provider's supply chain. Equally, once you have fully understood your supply chain and know how to maximize value at lowest cost, perhaps that supplier is no longer the best to meet your needs.

I would urge you wherever possible to undertake this type of analysis as soon as you can when you are embarking on a sourcing process. Then you can make more informed choices about the suppliers and the supply chain construct that best suit your needs. Obviously, if you are already in a long-term contract there is real value to be delivered by driving through this type of re-engineering project as a continuous improvement initiative. I am sure you can tell that I am a huge fan of this form of supply chain analysis, and I encourage you to embrace the technique wherever you are in the procurement cycle, as I am convinced it is capable of adding value at any point.

Safeguarding value

It is all too easy when you are trying to optimize costs to erode value. As we discussed earlier, the organization only acquires pencils because they are needed and therefore, as you re-engineer the supply chain, it is as important to safeguard value as it is to reduce cost.

Figure 19.4   Basic supply chain for goods and services

Figure 19.4 shows the basic supply chain for goods and services an organization will buy. When looking at the activities that add value to the supply chain, you should ask yourself what the activity contributes to the value proposition of the supply chain. In the example of the pencils supply chain the proposition could be: 'To provide staff members with a writing instrument whose output is erasable at lowest total cost while meeting health, safety and environmental objectives.' How important is the activity of *design* to the delivery of this objective? I suggest that it is probably important to the pencil manufacturer but not to either the stationery provider or the client. *Specifying* what the organization needs is important – particularly if this activity is used to standardize the requirement and reduce the varieties on offer. *Acquisition* is important because you can put in place a slick call-off process with automated payment that will take 90 per cent off the typical processing costs. *Use* is important because this is the heart of the matter and the whole reason you are buying the pencils. *Disposal* probably isn't important unless there are environmental issues to consider. From this simple example you will see that at least one if not two of the activities are unimportant to delivering value (ie design and disposal). If you have any costs devoted to these activities, I suggest you shut them down straight away and concentrate on the others that contribute to your value proposition.

No one likes variety

While I am on my hobby horse, I would just like to explode a popular myth – that suppliers like non-standard equipment or services. When I was working in the oil industry, I assumed that when our engineers designed non-standard pieces of equipment the suppliers loved it because they could charge premium prices. 'Enhancements' were endemic by the way, to the point where we used to play a game of spot-the-compressor – by the time the engineers had finished tweaking the standard design, it was almost impossible to make out the compressor underneath all the extra widgets. In fact the suppliers hated non-standard items because they had to re-tool their production line and order in lots of one-offs. This meant that while they did indeed charge more money for bespoke equipment, they actually lost margin as it was much more profitable for them to churn out their 'any colour as long as it's black' standards.

Aeroplanes and airlines

The process that applies to pencils also applies to aircraft and airlines; it just happens to be on a rather larger scale. It appears at least superficially rather similar, as you can see in Figure 19.5.

Aircraft manufacturer

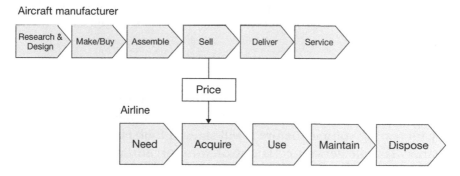

Figure 19.5 Aircraft supply chain

Let's look first at the airline's supply chain. When the airline is calculating its requirements it will be looking at its current fleet as well as its future capacity. For example, one of the reasons that Boeing is doing better with sales of its new freight plane than the competition is that its customers know that the spares and know-how of their current fleets of

747 are transferable. The airline will look at its current and forecast routes, passenger demand, etc and run various scenarios to cover economic, environmental and regulatory projections. All of this will help it to determine whether or not it needs to acquire new planes.

When it starts to look at the make and model of plane it should buy, the airline will consider factors such as the acquisition cost together with life-time costs like aircraft availability and reliability; maintenance routines and the cost and accessibility of spares; versatility (whether the planes can fly all the routes); attractiveness and quality of customer experience; fuel efficiency, economic life expectancy and resale value. All of these factors are captured in the supply chain under the headings of 'acquire', 'use', 'maintain' and 'dispose'.

Similarly, for aircraft manufacturers, all the activities of the supply chain hold true. They are just on a totally different scale. If you look at the supply chain for the Airbus 380 with its multi-country manufacturing and assembly model, which necessitated bespoke Airbus roll-on roll-off ferries, specially constructed barges, widened canals and strengthened roads, the relative scale and complexity of the operation is rather underplayed in the supply chain activity typically labelled 'Move'.

Obviously, if you were to optimize the supply chains associated with anything as complex as an aeroplane, its customers, manufacturers and the myriad suppliers that will be involved, it could take you years to complete. However, the processes and techniques are fundamentally the same as those you might use for a pencil (honest).

In summary

Negotiating a low price will only get you so far in reducing your costs – there is only so much you can take out of a supplier's margin, even by increasing volume, before it will start to look elsewhere to sell its wares. To take serious costs out of your organization you need to understand your total cost, which includes the purchase price but also all your internal costs. Armed with the total cost and your analysis of where your costs are incurred, you can open a dialogue with the supplier to look at re-engineering the supply chain. The aim of re-engineering is to 'shrink the pie' and reduce the total cost of the supply chain for both you and the supplier, reducing cost for you and potentially improving margins for the supplier. Once you understand the techniques you can apply them to all things great and small, complex and simple.

20 Keeping procurement on the agenda

Proving the value (again)

By now you are probably thinking that good procurement is like the proverbial painting of the Forth Rail Bridge in Scotland – never-ending. And actually you aren't far wrong in this assumption. As I have mentioned before, procurement is not rocket science, it is just very difficult to do it well, and even in organizations that are already doing procurement well, their greatest challenge is to keep doing it well.

This is partly due to human nature. Most of us get bored doing things over and over again. This is also partly the nature of business, where the priorities change or evolve and, where when something appears to be 'fixed', attention strays to the next opportunity. Another reason is that as good procurement practice becomes embedded in everyday business then its value proposition changes. Whereas in the early days of procurement improvement you could take double-digit savings out of your third-party expenditure while also improving the quality delivered and the customer value proposition as well as reducing time to market, now success might mean resisting inflationary pressures and maintaining service levels. But it doesn't need to be like that.

This is why, when the procurement transformation is complete, the headline improvements have been reported to the stock market and great performance has been rewarded, it is the time that procurement needs to work hardest and be most creative. Therefore in this chapter we are going to figure out how to keep doing great procurement and keep it at the top of the business agenda.

Demonstrating value

The first thing that you need to do to keep at the top of the agenda is to get there in the first place. If your colleagues do not think that the original procurement programme was an unadulterated success then it will be very difficult to keep them onside over the longer term. So, the first thing I want to cover in this chapter is how to demonstrate value and ensure everyone recognizes it. The best way to do this is to baseline, measure and report the improvements.

I ran a programme a few years ago that had a double ambition. The executive wanted to create a pan-organizational pot of money that could be used to fund a variety of projects across the company and felt that a cost reduction in its third-party expenditure was a good way to release the funds to fill the pot. At the start of the programme, my team calculated what savings could be delivered across the various divisions and business units through better procurement. Then, using this information, the company's finance department cut business budgets by the same amounts. The money from the budgets then went into the pan-organizational pot and my team worked alongside the businesses to help them do what they needed to for a lower cost against their reduced budgets.

This approach worked well for a variety of reasons. First, it can be very difficult to prove that cost has been saved because, if unchecked, it is easy for the business to just spend the extra money and therefore any impact on the bottom line is lost. By cutting budgets and transferring the freed-up funds this could not happen. Second, the business wanted to draw on the investment pot for its own projects and therefore had an additional incentive to make sure that the procurement improvement programme worked. Finally, the organization benefited from both short- and longer-term value improvement (the early benefits from procurement initiatives and the longer-term from the projects funded from the investment pot).

As with the case of Chrysler mentioned earlier in this book, measurement of cost reduction is critical to the credibility of any procurement programme. Therefore, in the example above, we established very clear rules about what counted as a benefit and what didn't, and created a rigorous audit process run partly by the finance department and ultimately by the budget holders in the business, who signed off the benefits. The programme only counted and reported those benefits that were capable of impacting the profitability of the organization, and other benefits such as cost avoidance were treated as memorandum items only.

These factors alone gave the procurement programme credibility across the organization and created a positive atmosphere in which business people actively sought to involve my team early in any sourcing project. The death knell of too many procurement projects has been sounded when the procurement director stands up in the boardroom and claims to have 'saved £100 million this year', and the finance director stands up and says, 'Show me where it's hit the bottom line.'

Initially the savings formula is likely to be simple, for example unit cost multiplied by expected volume. However, over time you will need more complex calculations. As you become more expert at understanding supply chains and total cost, your longer-term ambitions should be to refine and baseline costs to the point where you know the unit and marginal cost of the things that are important to you (I am not suggesting you boil the ocean here). This will allow you to track the impact on your organization of better management of your total cost base – the full sandpit of your own and third-party spend – and use this information to make and implement the best sourcing decisions. In this way you will move to a world of cost leadership where procurement is just one of the many disciplines your company excels in.

Holding the gain

As you will have recognized from everything that I have mentioned in the book so far, early cost reduction is a doddle and anyone can do it. The CEO can dry up third-party expenditure purely by claiming to be 'interested in it' and prices, if not always cost, can tumble after a few stern conversations with your suppliers.

The challenge is not so much to take cost out but to keep it out. As someone recently said to me, 'This isn't about the first £50 million savings, it's about the last.' This is so true, whether it's the last £50 million or £50, it will be much more difficult to achieve if the procurement department isn't world class, if the business is cynical and unengaged, if the management information and systems are creaky, if the sourcing decisions taken to date have been sloppy, and if inferior contracts have been left with middling suppliers for average goods or services.

Therefore, whenever you embark on a procurement programme of any kind it is always sensible to make sure that your funding will not only cover the cost reduction exercise but also allow you to upskill the procurement team and improve their systems, processes and management information. When the programme is delivering a return of 10:1 to the organization then there is likely to be a much greater appetite to invest a bit more at that point than later on when the going gets tougher and the returns are slimmer.

So it is important that the organization doesn't just complete the improvement exercise, get the T-shirt and move on to the next project, at least not without making sure that the most important of the new techniques, skills and processes are well embedded across the organization. Therein lies madness or – if you force me to be less poetic – at least a hockey stick-shaped upswing in your cost base at some point in the next few years as all the good work the organization has done unwinds.

Extended enterprise

We have already established that it is likely that at least half of the direct costs in any company, regardless of which industry it is in or how mature the company is, will be spent with its suppliers, and that these suppliers will have some responsibility for delivering the company's promises and value proposition. This being so, another of the key areas to invest in during your procurement programme is supplier and contract management. As already mentioned, there is no actual value delivered until the good or service you are buying is being used, and equally there is no value delivered in a contract until the supplier is delivering the good or service in the way the contract intended. Supplier and contract management is something that you should invest in from day one.

It also provides part of the answer to the conundrum being addressed in this chapter: how you keep delivering real value through good procurement over the longer term – because supplier and contract management, combined with commercial acumen, will be the route to continuous improvement and shrinking the pie. Once you have put in place the contract that rewards suppliers for what you value, you can start working with them to improve their service through changes to both your practices and theirs.

Mobilizing the whole organization

No matter how large or efficient the procurement team are, they are always likely to be a tiny fraction of the workforce. Therefore if you are determined to hold the gains of any procurement improvement it is important that the whole company starts to become more aware of its role in the better management of third-party spend and key suppliers, and the positive impact that it can have on the company's short- and long-term commercial health.

This is at the heart of creating a procurement proficient organization where informed managers sign appropriate contracts, business users ensure that key suppliers delight their customers and colleagues, and fit-for-purpose goods and services are acquired at all levels, with spend channelled through good company-wide contracts. Procurement proficiency needs boardroom commitment, slick systems and processes that deliver timely information into the hands of the commercial decision makers, and recognition across the organization that effective management of suppliers and spend is vital to the company's success. It delivers sustainable benefits in a way that no other procurement improvement lever can do. It demands a sophisticated balance of federalism and subsidiarity: where pan-company suppliers, goods and services are effectively managed for the greater good while activities and decisions best made locally are completed with commercial aplomb.

Total cost

To create a truly procurement proficient organization, the whole company must understand total cost. It must recognize that success is measured by the lifetime cost of a good or service and not by its price, and that the optimization of a function must be achieved in the context of the success of the supply chains it serves.

Total cost optimization requires cross-functional working to ensure that the business priority is the supply chain. These cross-functional teams could be in place for years and will require a strong matrix management capability across the organization, with multiple reporting lines. The importance of cross-functional working, where specialists are brought together to optimize the customer value proposition, cannot be overestimated. It creates an innovative yet focused environment to both solve problems and add worth.

Executive sponsorship

I hope that what you have read in this book will have convinced you that procurement is too important to be left to the procurement department and instead is something that merits board-level attention. This is most obvious when you are figuring out what your customer value proposition will be and remains true as you design your supply chain and select your key suppliers. Arguably, it is equally apparent when you want to reduce your third-party expenditure to improve your business performance, get the most out of a merger or acquisition, or share the pain of an economic or market downturn. However, executive sponsorship is probably less obvious but actually more important when you have made the initial changes, delivered the expected value, increased your market share or sailed into calmer economic waters. It might require less time in your diary but it does require the same level of visible commitment.

Good procurement, especially sustained good procurement, is not rocket science but it is difficult to deliver because of all the moving parts, competing interests, changing agendas and organizational constructs. It is much easier to achieve with your support. Thank you.

Glossary

bedrock pricing   A price recognized as the fair economic value of an item, based on the cost of the item plus an acceptable margin for the supplier.

benchmark   A measure of performance of your organization in comparison with other organizations or markets.

bottleneck   A term used to describe those items that are critical to the business where the organization has little leverage with the supplier.

category   A grouping of similar goods or services that enables an organization to analyse its spend.

client   The recipient of products or services from a supplier.

colleague   The recipient of the outcome of a supply chain who is internal to your organization.

consequential supply chain analysis   A technique for optimizing interrelated supply chains such that the most important of them (the primary supply chain) is not compromised by optimization made to subordinate supply chains.

core business activities   Those activities that are critical to a company's customer value proposition.

customer   The recipient of the outcome of a supply chain who is external to your organization.

customer value proposition   The functions and attributes of the product or service your organization supplies that your customers value because it enables them to do what they do faster, better or cheaper.

direct expenditure   Expenditure on goods and services acquired to be part of the good or service being created for sale.

enabling expenditure   Expenditure on goods and services being acquired to allow the organization to fulfil its customer value propositions but that don't as such go into the goods or services being sold.

feature   An attribute of a product or service that might help the customer select between two competing products (eg metallic paint or a sunroof in a car).

function   An attribute of a product or service that it must have for it to function, something that is intrinsic to the article (eg a car must have propulsion and something to sit on).

gainshare   The mechanism for sharing cost reductions between the client and its suppliers.

indirect expenditure   Expenditure on goods and services being acquired to support the business.

leverage   A term used to describe those items on which you spend a substantial amount of money and which are not business critical.

maverick buying   Refers to the situation where someone within the client organization does not buy from the preferred suppliers with agreed contracts.

monopoly supplier   A supplier who has a dominant position in a market, restricting client organization choice.

payment by results (PBR)   A contractual reward mechanism whereby what the client pays depends on the level of success of the outcome that the client derives from the services provided by the supplier.

price   The amount paid to the suppliers.

primary supply chain   The activities undertaken by the organization and its suppliers to deliver the customer value proposition. **Secondary supply chains** are subordinate to the primary supply chain and can be defined and optimized in their own right but will deliver most value when this is done in the context of the primary supply chain. *See also* consequential supply chain analysis.

procurement proficiency   When everyone involved in the activity of procurement understands the fundamentals of good procurement and is supported through effective management information and systems.

routine A term used to describe those items where you don't have much influence in the market and that are not business critical.

strategic A term used to describe those items where you have a significant market influence and that are business critical.

strategic alliance A collaborative relationship between a client and a supplier that furthers the strategic business ambitions of both.

supplier management The activity of managing suppliers and key contracts to ensure that they deliver the agreed value to the business.

supply chain A series of activities undertaken by a number of entities both internal and external to the organization that deliver an outcome to a customer or a colleague.

switching costs The costs involved in changing from an incumbent supplier to a new supplier.

third-party spend or expenditure Money being paid to other companies in return for goods and services.

tier one suppliers Those suppliers with whom you have a direct contractual relationship. **Tier two suppliers** would be those suppliers that have a contractual relationship with your tier one supplier from which you benefit.

total cost of ownership Comprises the life-time costs of the good or service required by the business. This must include the interactions with, and goods/services provided by, suppliers and internal stakeholders involved at all points in the lifecycle (eg transport, storage, installation, maintenance and decommissioning). Value associated with total cost of ownership occurs at the time of use and refers to its contribution to the business need.

References

Allpar.com, *SCORE: Supplier Cost Reduction Effort,* http://www.allpar.com/corporate/score.html, accessed February 2010

Alumni Achievement Awards (2009) *A G Lafley, MBA 1977,* Harvard Business School, October

Blackwell, E (2009) *Boeing's Delays Show Supplier Perils,* TheStreet.com

Bonabeau, E and Meyer, C (2001) Swarm intelligence: A whole new way to think about business, *Harvard Business Review,* May

Bradshaw, T (2009) Competition and demanding clients hit WPP, *Financial Times,* 27 June

Braun, J *et al, Chrysler Corporation: Innovations in supply chain management,* University of Michigan Business School, http://www-personal.umich.edu/~afuah/cases/case3.html, accessed February 2010

Curtis, J (July 2000) Performance related pay, *The Guardian,* 24 July

Earle, G (2008) Obama: Put lipstick on a pig, it's still a pig, *New York Post,* 9 September

Eda, H and Shintoh, T (2002) *ARM CPU Core Dominates Mobile Market,* Nikkei Business Publications, Tokyo

Fairtrade (2009) *Facts and Figures,* Fairtrade Labelling Organisations International, http://www.fairtrade.net/contact-us.html

Ferrari, B (2009) Lessons of the Tata Nano and rethinking big three supply chains, *Supply Chain Matters,* 24 March

Gallo, C (2009) How Amazon's Bezos sparked demand for Kindle 2, *Business Week,* 24 February

Greenemeier, L (2001) EDS and Xerox end legal spat, extend outsourcing pact, *Information Week,* 3 December

Hannon, D (2007) *Ford's Supplier Strategy Proves Difficult,* Purchasing.com

Johnson, G and Scholes, K (1997) *Exploring Corporate Strategy, Text and Cases,* Prentice Hall, Harlow

Kraljic, P (1983) Purchasing must become supply management, *Harvard Business Review*, Sept–Oct 1983

Maslow, A H (1943) A theory of human motivation, *Psychological Review*, **50,** pp 370–96

Moulden, D and Hutchinson, P (2006) *Brilliant NLP*, Pearson Education, Harlow

Porter, M E (1985) *Competitive Advantage – Creating and sustaining superior performance*, The Free Press, New York

PPI (May 2009) *Auto Supplier Study*, Planning Perspectives Inc, New York

Ray, D (January 2008) *Tata Motors Unveils the People's Car*, Tata Motors Press Release

Roland Berger (2009) *Global Automotive Supplier Industry is Facing the Biggest Crisis Ever*, Roland Berger Strategy Consultants, http:// www.rolandberger.com/contact.html

Scanlon, J (2009) What can Tata's Nano teach Detroit?, *Business Week*, 18 March

Shillingford, J (2001) From the BBC Micro, little Acorns grew, *The Guardian*, 8 March

Simons, J A, Irwin, DB and Drinnien, B A (1987) *Psychology – The search for understanding*, West Publishing Company, New York

Sorkin, A R (2000) Fashionmall.com swoops in for the Boo.com fire sale, *New York Times*, 2 June

Strassmann, P A (2000) The Xerox tragedy, *Computerworld*, November

Sturgeon, W (2002) *Technologies Time Forgot: The Acorn Electron*, Silicon. com, 18 January

Vise, D A (2005) *The Google Story*, Bantam Dell Publishing, New York

Ward, K (1993) *Corporate Financial Strategy*, Butterworth-Heinemann, Oxford

WPP (2009) *Annual General Meeting Trading Update for First Four Months of 2009*, WPPP, New York

WRAP (2009) *Case Studies: Courtauld commitment*, WRAP, Banbury (http://www.wrap.org.uk/downloads/CC_Case_Studies_16_dec_2009_final1.7a247242.6249.pdf)

Zasky, J (2003) Cool customer: Frederic Tudor and the frozen water trade, *Failure Magazine*, April

Index